MACMILLAN MASTER GUIDES

ANIMAL FARM BY
GEORGE ORWELL

MACMILLAN MASTER GUIDES

GENERAL EDITOR: JAMES GIBSON

JANE AUSTEN	*Emma* Norman Page
	Sense and Sensibility Judy Simons
	Persuasion Judy Simons
	Pride and Prejudice Raymond Wilson
	Mansfield Park Richard Wirdnam
SAMUEL BECKETT	*Waiting for Godot* Jennifer Birkett
WILLIAM BLAKE	*Songs of Innocence and Songs of Experience* Alan Tomlinson
ROBERT BOLT	*A Man for All Seasons* Leonard Smith
CHARLOTTE BRONTË	*Jane Eyre* Robert Miles
EMILY BRONTË	*Wuthering Heights* Hilda D. Spear
JOHN BUNYAN	*The Pilgrim's Progress* Beatrice Batson
GEOFFREY CHAUCER	*The Miller's Tale* Michael Alexander
	The Pardoner's Tale Geoffrey Lester
	The Wife of Bath's Tale Nicholas Marsh
	The Knight's Tale Anne Samson
	The Prologue to the Canterbury Tales Nigel Thomas and Richard Swan
JOSEPH CONRAD	*The Secret Agent* Andrew Mayne
CHARLES DICKENS	*Bleak House* Dennis Butts
	Great Expectations Dennis Butts
	Hard Times Norman Page
GEORGE ELIOT	*Middlemarch* Graham Handley
	Silas Marner Graham Handley
	The Mill on the Floss Helen Wheeler
T. S. ELIOT	*Murder in the Cathedral* Paul Lapworth
	Selected Poems Andrew Swarbrick
HENRY FIELDING	*Joseph Andrews* Trevor Johnson
E. M. FORSTER	*A Passage to India* Hilda D. Spear
	Howards End Ian Milligan
WILLIAM GOLDING	*The Spire* Rosemary Sumner
	Lord of the Flies Raymond Wilson
OLIVER GOLDSMITH	*She Stoops to Conquer* Paul Ranger
THOMAS HARDY	*The Mayor of Casterbridge* Ray Evans
	Tess of the d'Urbervilles James Gibson
	Far from the Madding Crowd Colin Temblett-Wood
BEN JONSON	*Volpone* Michael Stout
JOHN KEATS	*Selected Poems* John Garrett
RUDYARD KIPLING	*Kim* Leonée Ormond
PHILIP LARKIN	*The Less Deceived* and *The Whitsun Weddings* Andrew Swarbrick

MACMILLAN MASTER GUIDES

ANIMAL FARM BY

GEORGE ORWELL

JEAN ARMSTRONG

MACMILLAN

First published 1985 by
THE MACMILLAN PRESS LTD
Houndmills, Basingstoke, Hampshire RG21 2XS
and London
Companies and representatives
throughout the world

ISBN 0–333–38277–3

British Library Cataloguing in Publication Data
Armstrong, Jean
Animal Farm by George Orwell.—(Macmillan
master guides)
1. Orwell, George. Animal Farm
I. Title
823′.912   PR6029.R8A7
ISBN 0–333–38277–3
ISBN 0–333–39299–X export

11 10   9   8   7   6   5   4   3
03 02 01 00 99 98 97 96 95 94

Printed in Malaysia

CONTENTS

GENERAL EDITOR'S PREFACE

The aim of the Macmillan Master Guides is to help you to appreciate the book you are studying by providing information about it and by suggesting ways of reading and thinking about it which will lead to a fuller understanding. The section on the writer's life and background has been designed to illustrate those aspects of the writer's life which have influenced the work, and to place it in its personal and literary context. The summaries and critical commentary are of special importance in that each brief summary of the action is followed by an examination of the significant critical points. The space which might have been given to repetitive explanatory notes has been devoted to a detailed analysis of the kind of passage which might confront you in an examination. Literary criticism is concerned with both the broader aspects of the work being studied and with its detail. The ideas which meet us in reading a great work of literature, and their relevance to us today, are an essential part of our study, and our Guides look at the thought of their subject in some detail. But just as essential is the craft with which the writer has constructed his work of art, and this is considered under several technical headings – characterisation, language, style and stagecraft.

The authors of these Guides are all teachers and writers of wide experience, and they have chosen to write about books they admire and know well in the belief that they can communicate their admiration to you. But you yourself must read and know intimately the book you are studying. No one can do that for you. You should see this book as a lamppost. Use it to shed light, not to lean against. If you know your text and know what it is saying about life, and how it says it, then you will enjoy it, and there is no better way of passing an examination in literature.

JAMES GIBSON

GEORGE ORWELL'S WORKS

IN ORDER OF

PUBLICATION

Down and Out in Paris and London	1933
Burmese Days	1934
A Clergyman's Daughter	1935
Keep the Aspidistra Flying	1936
The Road to Wigan Pier	1937
Homage to Catalonia	1938
Coming up for Air	1939
Inside the Whale and other essays	1940
The Lion and the Unicorn	1941
Animal Farm	1945
Critical Essays	1946
The English People	1947
Nineteen Eighty Four	1949
Shooting An Elephant and other essays	1950
Collected Essays	1953
Decline of the English Murder and other Essays	1961
The Collected Essays, Journalism and Letters of George Orwell (ed. Sonia Orwell and Ian Angus)	1968

Collected and published after Orwell's death

ACKNOWLEDGEMENTS

The editor and publishers are grateful to A. M. Heath Limited on behalf of the estate of the late Mrs Sonia Brownell Orwell, and Secker & Warburg Limited for permission to reproduce extracts from the works of George Orwell.

Cover illustration: *Three Prize Pigs Outside a Sty*, English School, courtesy of Iona Antiques, London, and the Bridgeman Art Library.

1 THE MAN AND HIS WORK

George Orwell's real name was Eric Blair. The name by which he became known as one of the century's foremost writers was adopted when *Down and Out in London and Paris* (1933), his first book, was about to be published. George Orwell was one of several pseudonymns that he suggested but it does have a particularly appropriate English flavour which suits his work – Orwell is the name of an English river and George is England's patron saint. For convenience I will be referring to him as Orwell.

He was born on 25 June 1903 in Motihari, Bengal when his father was in the Indian Civil Service and it was here that he spent his earliest years. When he was four the family returned to England to settle at Henley on Thames, a popular place for returning colonials, but Orwell's father, having settled his family, returned to India until he retired some years later. In his essay 'Why I Write' Orwell says:

> I was the middle child of three but there was a gap of five years on either side and I barely saw my father before I was eight. For this and other reasons I was somewhat lonely. . .I had the lonely child's habit of making up stories and holding conversations with imaginary persons.

Very early, then, he was acquiring that habit of mind which would later develop into a tendency to sustain a continuous narrative in his head, describing what he saw to himself although he did not write it down.

When he was five he went to the local primary school, was recommended for a scholarship to a preparatory school and, being successful, was sent to St Cyprian's at Eastbourne on the south coast. We can read a retrospective account of his time here in the essay 'Such, Such Were the Joys' (1952) but we must take care not to accept it as entirely auto-biographical. It is an account of a very unhappy time in his life and may be looked at as an emotional account rather than a factual one. However, throughout a study of Orwell the reader should be on his guard and remember it is Orwell's skill as a writer we should be appreciating and not his integrity as a reporter. Much of his work is based on personal experience and a lot of this was deliberately used in his work to make a moral or political point. To do this he may well have distorted the facts – adopting a pose, selecting only what was relevant to support his point, or reinterpreting the past in the light of later ideas.

From St Cyprian's Orwell won a scholarship to a public school, Wellington College, when he was thirteen. After a year he went on to Eton as a King's Scholar. He wrote no essay recording this time in his life and, indeed, referred to it later as 'five years in a lukewarm bath of snobbery'. He was popular here, however, unlike St Cyprian's, and took part in the general life of the school where the post-war cynicism and disenchantment that was prevalent at the time probably corresponded to something in his own nature. He was no longer the outsider, as he had felt himself to be at his preparatory school.

After Eton, Orwell did not go on to university. He did not much enjoy academic life and had not put himself out to work very hard at Eton, but in *Keep the Aspidistra Flying* (1936) he has Comstock, an unsuccessful writer working in a dingy bookshop, refer contemptuously, but also with bitterness and envy, to the bright young Oxbridge graduates who write their slim volumes with such ease, having all the right connections to succeed. While we must not assume that Comstock is Orwell, the latter did himself work in a bookshop while a struggling and not yet successful writer, so the ambiguous attitude to university life and the privileges it gave one, which Comstock expresses, could be his own. His father suggested the Indian Civil Service as a career and Orwell, wishing to return to the East, settled upon the Indian Imperial Police, was accepted as a candidate, chose to return to Burma, was selected and went out on 22 October 1922.

Episodes from his journey out were recalled much later to be written as articles for the socialist journal *Tribune* and, as Professor Crick points out in *George Orwell*, which is as much a critical analysis as a biography, these demonstrate his technique of reinterpreting experience in the light of later ideas. One of the episodes – about a quartermaster who is 'scurrying like a rat' to conceal the food he has stolen – is given a socialist perspective. Does the quartermaster, surrounded by overfed bourgeois and *nouveaux riches*, need to steal food? The other - about one of 'a swarm of coolies' who gets a kick in the backside - is given a racialist perspective. This was how one expected to treat the natives. It is interesting too that animal metaphors are used: the quartermaster is a 'rat' and the coolie is part of a 'swarm', both metaphors containing value judgements. The natives were also presented as the victims in his book *Burmese Days* (1934), which is based on his experiences in Burma. They are presented as being exploited and mistreated by the 'pukka sahibs', a class he refers to as 'dull, boozing, witless porkers'. This novel was written some ten years before *Animal Farm* and shows us that Orwell had for a long time associated pigs with exploitation and the abuse of power. In *Down and Out in Paris and London* (1933) we can find the precursor of Squealer in *Animal Farm* - Charlie, who can turn black into white just as Squealer can. The roots of the fable go deep.

Orwell served in Upper Burma from 1922-7 and he appears to have been horrified by the role he was obliged to play and ended up by hating imperialism and the behaviour it demanded of him. His ambivalent position is succinctly portrayed in the essay 'Shooting an Elephant' (1937). Full of hatred for imperialism and autocracy of any kind, Orwell returned home to England from his untenable position where he had seen 'the dirty work of Empire at close quarters'. He returned with a strong psychological distrust of authority reinforcing what he had felt in his schooldays. 'The Hanging' is another important essay based on this time and admirably demonstrates Orwell's technique of marrying reported experience with recollection. It is well worth reading by a student exploring Orwell's attitude to authority, power and exploitation.

Back in England, Orwell settled down to try and write. He spent much of his time experimentally among tramps and down-and-outs, trying to find out at first hand what life was like for those who were 'victims' in England. In the spring of 1928 he went to Paris where he attempted articles, short stories and two novels, but could get nothing published. Eventually he ran out of money and took a job as a dishwasher in a smart hotel on the Rue de Rivoli, using these experiences and those of his tramping days in England as the basis of his first book which was eventually published through the intervention of a friend after he had abandoned it.

After his time in Paris he returned to England to a job tutoring a retarded boy, picking hops in Kent and teaching in private schools, these last two experiences giving him material for *A Clergyman's*

Daughter (1935). He began reviewing for the journal *Adelphi* and took a job in a Hampstead bookshop.

In January 1936 he was commissioned to write a book about the unemployed in the north of England and he went north, living in the houses of working-class people to research for this book which became *The Road to Wigan Pier* (1937). He began to awaken as a political thinker, hearing the theories he had read about being discussed by self-educated working men. He also saw the effects of the class system in action:

> In order that Hitler may march the goosestep, that the Pope may denounce Bolshevism, that the cricket crowds may assemble at Lords, that the poets may scratch one another's back, coal has got to be forthcoming.

This comment, placed after a vivid description of the punishing job of the coal-miner which can be read separately as the essay 'Down the Mine' (1940), demonstrates Orwell's skill at polemic, which is any form of vigorous argument, controversy or dispute, usually social, political or religious.

Orwell was mixing at the time with the most politically conscious section of the working class, mainly Marxists of one persuasion or another. From Wigan he moved to Barnsley where he heard Oswald Mosley expounding Fascist ideas totally at variance with Marxist ideology. He notes that Mosley was a very good speaker and comments – (something he was to make the central issue of *Animal Farm*):

> It struck me how easy it is to bamboozle an uneducated audience if you have prepared beforehand a set of repartees with which to evade questions.

One can almost hear Squealer in *Animal Farm*, who replies to all awkward questions 'surely you do not want Jones back?' Orwell came back from his visit to the North convinced that society could be rearranged for the better.

When he returned he set up home at Wallington, a village in Hertfordshire – he married during this time – and kept the farmyard animals that he presents in *Animal Farm*. But he was not to remain here long as the Spanish Civil War (1936–9) had broken out and over two thousand British enlisted in the International Brigade and left-wing sympathisers everywhere supported the Republican government against the Fascist forces led by General Franco. Orwell joined the small dissident Marxist group POUM (Workers Party for Marxist Unity) which was one of the groups working for revolution. He was wounded in Spain but came out of hospital to find that POUM had been declared illegal and many of his comrades had been imprisoned or shot. The Soviet Union, although ideologically opposed to Fascism, did not want to encourage a workers' revolution so near the French border and jeopardise their French alliance. It was this turn-about that made Orwell so bitter about revolution. Many of his friends had disappeared, betrayed by those with whom they had been fighting for the same cause, declared Fascist supporters by the Communists they had been fighting with against Franco. Orwell managed to escape and on returning to England he wanted to inform the public of the cynicism of the Stalinists who were interested only in the development of Russia and their own political careers rather than in international socialism which was the aim of Marxism. He wanted to expose the betrayed revolution but nobody wanted to listen. He had to read the distorted versions in the newspapers and could no nothing to put things right. 'It gives me the feeling the very concept of objective truth is fading out of the world', he wrote 'Lies will pass into history.' The novel *Homage to Catalonia* (1938) presents his version of what happened but it passed almost unnoticed, to his intense disappointment. He had to find a way of reaching the public with a political allegory everybody would understand. This was eventually to be *Animal Farm*.

After his return from Spain he spent some time in a santorium where tuberculosis was diagnosed and he wintered in Morocco where he wrote a nostalgic book *Coming up for Air* (1939). When the Second Word War broke out he was again at Wallington and writing essays. *Inside the Whale* (1940) was his first book of collected essays.

He tried to join the army but was refused because of his health so he moved to London where he joined the Home Guard, reviewed films and plays and wrote book reviews for *Tribune*. In 1941 he joined the Eastern department of the BBC where he broadcast talks to India but he was greatly frustrated by the bureaucracy and found the propaganda put over the air distasteful. The idea of the Ministry of Truth in *Nineteen Eighty Four* (1949) may be rooted in this time. Winston Smith is tortured in Room 101 of the Ministry of Love – at the BBC Orwell worked in Room 101! He resigned and became Literary Editor of *Tribune* in which he had a weekly column where he sometimes offended his more doctrinaire socialist readers. He also began to pull together his ideas for *Animal Farm*.

Since the Spanish Civil War socialists had been looking more and more towards the Soviet Union for leadership and Stalin was eventually regarded as a friend and ally against Hitler, so this was not an opportune time to produce a devastating criticism of the Soviet Union or a brilliant exposition of the pursuit of power. Orwell was horrified at the way propaganda had duped the British public and he was determined not to stand by and do nothing when British publishers, afraid of offending public opinion, refused to publish *Animal Farm*. He maintained, 'If liberty means anything at all it means the right to tell people what they do not want to hear.' Eventually Secker and Warburg agreed to publish the book but not until Orwell, losing heart, had begun arrangements to publish it himself as a pamphlet. *Animal Farm* became an immediate best-seller and was eventually translated into over thirty languages. At last Orwell had got the hearing he wanted.

At the end of the war, after he and his wife had adopted a baby, Orwell's wife died during an operation and Orwell went with his son to live on Jura, an island in the Inner Hebrides and a most unsuitable environment for a man with tuberculosis. Here, struggling against his disease, he wrote his last novel, *Nineteen Eighty Four*, a most pessimistic last testament in which his faith in 'decency' and the working classes has quite withered away. In *Animal Farm* the pigs grab power and get the best out of life for themselves but in *Nineteen Eighty Four* this is pushed even further – power is not a means to an end but is an end in itself.

Orwell remarried but died in London early in 1950, exhausted by his work and his disease, but since his death he continues to get his 'hearing' and has come to be regarded as one of the twentieth century's foremost writers.

2 THE CHOICE OF A FORM

In 'Why I Write' Orwell says, '*Animal Farm* was the first book in which I tried, with full consciousness of what I was doing, to fuse political purpose and artistic purpose into one whole.' He also says in the same essay that he had wanted for a long time to make political writing into an art. It is obvious, then, that after the disappointment of *Homage to Catalonia* he was searching for a way to get himself the hearing he wanted in a form that suited his purpose – primarily to expose the Stalinist regime in the Soviet Union, the betrayal of the 1917 October Revolution and, after his own experiences in the Spanish Civil War, his disenchantment with all revolutions.

With *Animal Farm* he found that form in the *satirical beast fable* which has a long literary history. We have seen that Orwell sometimes presented victims and their oppressors as animals and that he himself kept real animals, becoming, no doubt, familiar with their particular characteristics. At Wallington, after his return from Spain, he seems first to have had the idea of using animals to present a political idea. In the Preface to the Ukrainian edition of *Animal Farm* he tells us about the time he was watching a young boy driving an enormous cart-horse and comments, 'It struck me that if only such animals became aware of their strength we should have no power over them, and that men exploit animals in much the same way as the rich exploit the proletariat.' His understanding of animals through his own observation, his tendency occasionally to present characters with animal metaphors, and the insight that he states above, all combined to produce the fable – *Animal Farm* – that political allegory which everybody would, and did, understand.

2.1 FABLE

Most of you will be acquainted with the fables of Aesop and some of you may have read La Fontaine's verse renderings, the crisp dryness of which is apparent in Orwell's fable – that matter-of-fact tone and economic style. You will, no doubt, be aware of the origin of such sayings as 'it's just sour grapes' or 'slow and steady wins the race'. One of the slogans of *Animal Farm* has been adopted into common political currency in a similar way, 'All animals are equal but some animals are more equal than others'.

A fable is a moral tale usually, but not always, with animals as characters and a satirical beast fable is a form which uses animals to tell us something about human nature and institutions. In this form it is possible to gain a distance, to say things that could not otherwise be said to the same effect. An example is Book IV of Jonathan Swift's *Gulliver's Travels* that satire on human nature about an island inhabited by rational, talking horses and sub-human, degenerate creatures called Yahoos. Orwell was a great admirer of Swift, he read *Gulliver's Travels* over half a dozen times in his lifetime and said in one of the BBC broadcasts that no year went by without his re-reading at least some part of it. Orwell thought that Swift 'laid it on a bit thick', that his view of human nature was too pessimistic. Orwell believed that people were basically decent, that the ordinary man, left to himself – not duped with propaganda – would live in a reasonable, decent way, but this point of view is repudiated to some extent by *Animal Farm*, where the fault is seen to be not so much in the nature of revolutions as in human nature itself. Even more pessimistic is *Nineteen Eighty Four* where everything that is worth-while in human nature is to be crushed out and the quality of life kept artificially low.

A fable does have some distinguishing characteristics by which it can be identified from other forms of narrative. The characters, for example, are representative types, not fully rounded characters such as we would expect to find in a novel; they are abstractions, rather like chess pieces that are moved around to suit the intention of the author – the fox will always be crafty, the lion will always be King of the Beasts, the sheep will always be stupid, the pigs will always be piggishly egotistical. Orwell does present his characters as types with primary distinguishing qualities – the pigs are exploiters, the horses are labourers, the sheep are easily led, the pigeons are messengers, the dogs are trained to be vicious – but at the same time, to some extent, particular personalities are revealed as the narrative progresses and sometimes characters do evoke an emotional response.

Another characteristic of the fable form is that it reveals a concern with design; its shape can be admired for its own sake and part of the pleasure in reading a fable is the pleasure of discovering this design, its rhythms and counterpointing. This aspect of the fable contributed greatly to Orwell's desire that political purpose and artistic purpose should be fused; the balances and symmetries of the fable contribute not only to its aesthetic quality but enable Orwell to enforce the point he wants to make. Examples of design can be seen in the positive version of the Seven Commandments and their negative counterparts after they have been changed; in the counter-balancing of the scene from the hill in Chapter 2, where the animals gather the day after they have ousted Jones and express their pride and faith in a new life, with the scene in Chapter 7, where they creep away to the same hill after the terrible executions and remember that this was not what they had looked forward to when they fought for their freedom. Many, many examples can be found and the pleasure of finding them for oneself is well worth the effort. This aspect of the fable will be discussed in greater detail in the section 'Summaries, and Critical Commentaries.

A lightness of touch is another characteristic of the fable; by this I mean that there will no doubt be humour in some form or another – the comic or the burlesque perhaps (burlesque is a form of comic art characterised by ridiculous exaggeration) and the tone will be controlled so that however strongly the author wishes to make his point, and it is usually an ethical point, he does not do so in a straightforward, sermonising way but by controlling the tone so that the reader is often beguiled through stern lessons. Orwell certainly employs such devices in *Animal Farm*. For all its devastating satire the fable is a masterpiece of controlled tone and even when the most dreadful events are taking place Orwell manages to lighten the narrative by various devices. For example, when the confessions and executions are taking place – one of the most dreadful episodes of the book – we hear that two sheep have confessed to murdering an old ram, but this has been done by 'chasing him round and round a bonfire when he was suffering from a cough' which certainly has elements of the burlesque.

If the fable form was admirably suited to Orwell's purpose, it was also a form to which his technique readily adapted. In all his writings Orwell had a tendency to class people into types – societal types – and these appear in different forms in different books. For example, in

Burmese Days the pukka sahibs, those 'dull, boozing, witless porkers' who imposed themselves on the natives, were the exploiting class; in *Down and Out in Paris and London* this class is presented as the greedy restaurateurs and gorging bourgeois or *nouveaux riches*. In this first book of Orwell's we can see very well the representative types at work; they conform to their roles and let Orwell get on with his point without the undue intrusion of personality. Here we also have Squealer's precursor – a type Orwell particularly detested – we have Charlie, that strange character that Orwell reputedly meets in the local bistro in his quartier in Paris. Charlie was 'very pink and young', he had fresh cheeks and tiny feet, he had abnormally short arms and other suggestions of a pig-like appearance. He also 'had a way of dancing and capering while he talked as though he were too happy and too full of life to keep still for an instant. . .he declaimed like an orator. . .his small, rather piggy eyes glittered with enthusiasm. He was, somehow, profoundly disgusting to see.' This is Squealer in human form, Squealer who was a small, fat pig with very round cheeks, twinkling eyes and nimble movements. Squealer too is a brilliant talker and never stands still, 'when he was arguing some difficult point he had a way of skipping from side to side and whisking his tail.' The physical attractiveness of both is made clear only to be undermined by the revolting characters of both. Squealer is Napoleon's propaganda man: 'it was said of him that he could turn black into white', an attribute Charlie also possesses, for he declaims upon love, calling it 'the highest and most refined emotion' a human being can aspire to but the experience he is describing turns out to be the vicious rape of a peasant girl sold into slavery by her parents.

One of the things Orwell said about himself was that he was not a 'real novelist' and one of his weaknesses in this form is his characterisation. In the novels the characters are often unsatisfactory because they are being used to represent a type or to be the vehicle of an idea. In the fable form this is, of course, a positive asset. A fable cannot present complex personalities; everything must, in the end, be subordinated to the idea – the abstract – so while, for example, we may feel great sadness for Boxer our primary feeling is outrage at the way he has been treated. It is to the betrayal of the animals by their comrades, who previously fought beside them for the same end, that Orwell wishes to give the greatest impact, not to the particular ways that this betrayal was felt by individuals. The complexity of human emotions that the suffering of the animals could have evoked is carefully controlled so that the impact is sustained. We do not feel pity for the suffering so much as outrage at the injustice. *Animal Farm* can be seen to be a perfect example of the fable form; it exactly suits Orwell's purpose and by the exigencies of its nature the satire is sharpened to a lethal point. The fable's function is to make a moral point. It is a kind of game and a skilful fabulist moves his pieces in such a way that he 'wins' his point and it is seen to be inevitable within the rules of the game. When we read a fable we accept the terms of the narrative, the oversimplification, the limits previously agreed, just as when we play chess we accept the rules of the game and that different pieces move in specific ways.

It is this characteristic movement of the figures in a fable that make it less disturbing than a satire. In *Animal Farm* the fable can be combed out from other aspects of the book and we may agree that as a fable it is highly satisfactory when we are not so happy with, for example, the allegorical aspect. As a fable we can see early on that the conclusion is inevitable, for we accept that Boxer's blind loyalty and gullibility, for example, will move constantly in conjunction with Napoleon's intelligence and greed. We know that nothing will intervene to prevent the inevitable outcome, that no change or development in the characters will take place – for this is the nature of a fable. We must 'play the game' according to the rules and learn our lesson from the outcome. This is the traditional function of a fable. We must consider the attitudes and actions it presents and consider how these in combination bring about the conclusion, deciding in what way this could have been avoided. The purpose of reading a fable is not to accept passively the moral presented but to seek alternatives having decided why the conclusion happened the way it did.

2.2 SATIRE

It might be worth while to take a closer look at satire and define exactly what it is and exactly how it works before looking at its target. Satire is the art of criticising through ridicule or contempt and it makes use of many devices – invective, irony, the comic, the burlesque – to control its tone and, therefore, the point of view. The word 'satire' came into our language in the early sixteenth century but the rather narrow range of literary forms it covered then have since widened considerably. It is interesting to note that many early versions of the word 'poet' in different languages coincide with the word meaning 'to scoff' or 'to scold', which is what a satire does. The earliest English satires were probably 'disgrace poems' or 'disgrace songs'. Satire is evident in many languages and cultures and has a long literary history; the idea that a writer should use his pen as a weapon against an enemy, or as a scalpel exposing diseased tissue is not new.

For a satire to work two things are necessary. Firstly, the author must evolve a criticism of some human activity and present it in such a way that it can be readily understood and secondly, he must encourage the reader to adopt his point of view and accept it as his own. In a novel the narrative works best when a reader identifies with a character or characters, entering into empathetic understanding, feeling what the character is feeling. In a satire the narrative works if the reader can be brought to identify with the author, seeing with his eyes what the author is criticising. In order to persuade the reader to see things his way rather than immediately begin to argue to the contrary, the author needs to appeal to the reader, needs to win his sympathy by some device or another; he needs to appear amiable so that the reader is drawn to him, taking his side against a common enemy. As the content of the satire is criticism and the reader may not, when he begins to read, have anything at all in common with the author, the latter needs to walk a tightrope of literary devices if his object is to be attained. If he shouts too loudly in his anger, or is too vitriolic in his abuse, the reader might be frightened away, or simply irritated. Anger does not attract but repels – even if the reader felt the anger justified he would not, from observing it or being subjected to it by the author, transfer it to himself. The satirist needs to be in control; if he wants the reader to feel anger, he himself must be wary of expressing it.

Knowing this, it is easy to see why satire works in an indirect way and why we find in *Animal Farm* much that is humorous when the intention is of a serious nature. A direct attack may seem more honest, anger may seem sincere, but it is the indirect attack that will be most effective. With a direct approach you might lose half your readers with the first sentence. Seeing you to be good-natured (employing humorous devices) and without malice (not attacking a named object) the reader is likely to listen longer. This is what the satirist wants. By careful control of the narrative he can keep the object being criticised in front of the reader's vision, turning it this way and that so that different facets are seen, or certain areas or characteristics only are spotlighted, beguiling the reader with various literary devices so that he sees and criticises for himself rather than feeling that he has been persuaded or imposed upon. In the best satires the satirist and his readers are an elite – anyone who does not see as they see is a fool or a blind man. The reader has identified with the writer and the object is attained.

2.3 FAIRY TALE

Orwell subtitled *Animal Farm* 'A Fairy Story' and we might ask whether he meant any more than that it was, at its simplest level, a story that could be read and enjoyed by children in the way that traditional fairy tales can. At the fantasy level *Animal Farm* is a farmyard tale of much charm and pathos where badly treated animals, overthrowing their oppressors, working as hard as they can to create a new life for themselves, accepting new leaders from amongst themselves, end up no better off than they were in the beginning. At this level we can feel the injustice, the sense of being trapped and confused by forces that we cannot understand or control, we can feel the pathos of the animals' predicament and can look down the hillside with Clover, our eyes full of tears for the dream that has turned into a nightmare.

But *Animal Farm* is not a satisfactory fairy story – there is no recovery, no happy ending, no feeling that a good life is possible if only we were brave enough and good enough and persevered to overcome all obstacles. It does not have the therapeutic effect we expect from a fairy story, leading us from confusion and fear into recovery and resolution. In fact, *Animal Farm* does just the opposite – it does not reassure, it disturbs; it does not offer a solution, it suggests endless confusion; it does not hold out hope for the future but presents a final state of hopelessness. Even the 'culture-hero', the strong hardworking Boxer, is presented in contradiction, directing all his energies to the wrong end, inadvertently supporting his oppressor. Boxer is strong, we argue at fairy tale level, so why doesn't his friend Benjamin teach him to use his strength wisely? Why don't they get together and work out what is happening and do something about it? Is the last scene one of total hopelessness or will understanding now dawn on the animals, is this a turning point for them? When we read the story as a fairy tale all these questions and more are there to be answered. A satisfactory fairy story should have answered them.

It is more likely that the subtitle is intended to be in itself an ironic comment. All criticism of Joseph Stalin and communist Russia was, at the time it was published, suppressed. Stories telling of oppression and atrocities would no doubt have been dismissed as 'fairy tales' made up by 'oppositionists'. What actually went on in the Soviet Union never reached the ears of those outside it, instead propaganda – more 'fairy tales' – presented the régime in a favourable light. Orwell had tried to tell the public the truth but had been unable to get his articles published so his 'fairy story' was his way of playing the same game; hearing the truth classed as stories worthy only of credulous children and countered by even more fantastic stories, he was hoping that his book would adjust the balance.

The subtitle can be seen to be a beguiling device setting the tone of the book as well as, in retrospect, the wry comment that it is.

2.4 ALLEGORY

Allegory is a narrative in which events or people are presented symbolically so that a deeper meaning is carried by the narrative than the story it seems to be telling. Allegory is often used to teach a moral lesson.

On one level *Animal Farm* is a satiric allegory of Russian Communism, of that period between the Revolution of 1917 to the Teheran Conference of November 1943 (the month in which *Animal Farm* was begun) when Stalin the leader of the USSR met the leaders of the Western allies, Franklin Roosevelt and Winston Churchill, to discuss mutual aid against Adolf Hitler. Through allegory the 'Soviet myth' as Orwell saw it could be criticised from the distance that this device allowed. A direct attack in the form of polemic, of essay or article, was not possible. Orwell had tried but failed to get anything critical of the Soviet Union published because of the strong pro-Russian feeling in Britain at the time. Stalin had become, after the Teheran Conference, a friend and ally of the West. *Animal Farm* was written between November 1943 and February 1944 when this feeling was at its height.

Sometimes allegory is complex and subtle, sometimes it is a simplification. Orwell himself said of *Animal Farm*:

> Although various episodes are taken from the actual history of the Russian Revolution, they are dealt with schematically and their chronological order is changed.

Critics have responded in different ways to this aspect of the work, according to their reading of it and, no doubt, to their understanding and interpretation of the historical events and processes it presents.

Jeffrey Meyers in his essay on allegory in *A Readers Guide to George Orwell* (1975) states:

> The political allegory of *Animal Farm*, whether specific or general, detailed or allusive, is pervasive, thorough and accurate, and the brilliance of the book becomes much clearer when the satiric allegory is compared to the political actuality.

George Steiner in the *New Yorker* (1969) views the allegory rather differently. He acknowledges it but says

> as an analysis of Communist dictatorship, of Stalinist mental processes, it seems to me thin and, understandably, desperate.

A summary of the allegory follows and more detailed analysis is suggested in the section 'Summaries and Critical Commentaries'.

2.5 THE POLITICAL ALLEGORY OF *ANIMAL FARM*

The story opens with a gathering together of the animals of Manor Farm to hear what Old Major, the prize boar, has to tell them. He is near the end of his life and wants to pass on his thoughts and ideas, his dream of the future, and to teach the animals a revolutionary song called 'Beasts of England'. This is an allegory both for the bringing of Marxist ideas to Russia and Lenin's wish to teach the people about its principles and to unify the Social Democratic Party. Lenin (Vladimir Ilyích Ulyanov) was a Russian revolutionary politician who put Karl Marx's ideas into practice – Marx was a nineteenth-century economist, thinker and politician, and joint author of the *Communist Manifesto*. Old Major's speech to the animals is a neat summary of Marx's ideas, that conflict between classes, here animals and humans, was at the root of social ills – both groups having rival economic interests – and that until the exploited class (animals or proletariat) took control of the means of production they would never be free, being kept in bondage by a capitalist class who lived a privileged life on the profits of their labour. Old Major, following Marx and Lenin, sees revolution as the means by which the yoke of oppression would be thrown off.

The Rebellion on Manor Farm is an allegory for the Russian Revolution of 1917. Marx had argued that eventually the proletariat, or working classes, would rise and overthrow the capitalist class because capitalism could not survive and socialism would be the next stage in a historical progression from feudalism to communism. Under capitalism, the rich would get richer and the poor would get poorer, Marx argued. Because capitalism depended on the 'impoverishment of the workers' (*Das Kapital* (1867-94)), eventually the time would come when the poor would rebel, violently overthrowing the capitalist class, and there would follow a 'dictatorship of the proletariat' before this stage also passed away and a state of communism without the need for coercion ensued. Marx taught, and Old Major's speech echoes this, that the workers were kept in bondage because they were alienated from the products of their labour, working only for a wage while the profit went elsewhere. Only if the means of production were held in common would they be restored to their rightful place in society, and Marx's aim was to prepare the working classes of industrialised countries for a revolution that would bring this about. Marx was an internationalist and the *Communist Manifesto* (1848) concludes with the words 'Working men of all countries unite!', which is closely echoed at the end of Old Major's speech to the animals.

Revolutionary communism is based on these teachings of Marx as interpreted by Lenin, who was the driving force behind the Russian Revolution. In the story *Animal Farm*, Old Major represents both Marx and Lenin but it is well to remember Orwell's comments that the book is a schematic approach and that the allegory does not follow the chronological order of historical events.

In 1917 Lenin, leading the majority or Bolshevik Party, seized power from the Tsarist regime in the name of the people and the 'proletariat dictatorship' followed. This is represented in the story by the enforcement of the principles of Animalism (Communism). Snowball and Napoleon, the rivals for leadership in the new regime, are counterparts for Leon Trotsky and Joseph Stalin and the pigs represent the Bolsheviks, later called Communists. The 'dictatorship of the proletariat' was viewed by some, and it seems that Orwell held this point of view, as the dictatorship of the Bolshevik Party. In the story this is allegorised by the obvious supremacy of the pigs even at the beginning. While the farm is called 'Animal Farm' and there are 'Sunday Meetings' to discuss matters of policy, and while the principle 'all animals are equal' is upheld in theory, the pigs can be seen to be the new ruling class and affairs are arranged so that more and more power is in their hands. The Sunday discussions are eventually banned and the pigs form a committee which represents the Politburo, the highest decision-making body of the Communist Party. The animals are proud and happy, however, that they own their own farm and are deceived about their position, while the reader becomes aware that a new ruling class has developed. The principle 'all animals are equal' is being corrupted and revisions of earlier ideas, and even the doctrine of Animalism which is contained in the Seven Commandments, are being effected.

In the story, news of the Rebellion soon spreads and causes concern among the farmers who fear their own animals might follow suit, just as the rulers of adjacent countries were concerned after the Russian Revolution. The Battle of the Cowshed is an allegory for the Counter-revolution when supporters of the Tsar – the White Russians – attempted to seize back power assisted by military and financial aid from the West, which was concerned about the growth of Bolshevism. The leadership of the Communist Party, after Lenin's death, was contended for by Stalin and Trotsky who differed in their ideas about the growth of socialism and the development of Russia. Their differences are allegorised in the dispute about the building of the windmill. Trotsky wanted to pursue world revolution and international socialism while Stalin wanted to pursue socialism in one country only, developing Russian strength. Trotsky wanted to industrialise while Stalin was more concerned about collectivising the farms to supply food for the growing urban population. These differences are neatly allegorised by the slogans 'Vote for Snowball and the three day week' and 'Vote for Napoleon and the full manger'. Snowball's expulsion represents the exile of Trotsky by Stalin who became ruler of the USSR and eventually removed all who opposed him to maintain and strengthen his position. This is, of course, allegorised by the way Napoleon maintains and strengthens his position through fear and justifies his every action through Squealer, who is a living *Pravda*, the official Party newspaper.

The drive towards industrialisation that Stalin did eventually pursue (his name is derived from the Russian word for steel and one of his titles was Stalin the Industrialiser), and the Five Year Plans to develop Russian into an industrial nation, is allegorised by Napoleon's decision to build the windmill after all, together with all the difficulties that this entailed. As Stalin also pursued his collectivisation of the farms together with the development of industry, difficulties and hardships followed for the Russian people. There was a great famine and over three million people are reputed to have died as a direct result of his policies of the time. In *Animal Farm* these difficulties and hardships are allegorised by those of the animals – the shortage of food, the lack of time to plough and sow the fields, the threat of reduced rations. Snowball is used as a scapegoat, being blamed for everything that goes wrong to divert criticism from Napoleon and his policies, just as Trotsky was by Stalin. Shortages and failures were blamed on the sabotage of Trotsky's disciples.

In the story the pigs gradually acquire a privileged lifestyle. When the principles of animalism get in the way of what Napoleon wants to do, he changes them. This is, no doubt, an allegory for the revisions that were made to Lenin's interpretation of Marxism when Stalin was in power, principles giving way to expediency. All who question Napoleon are silenced either by Squealer's persuasive tactics (propaganda) or by fear. Eventually executions take place after those 'guilty' publicly confess their guilt, their allegiance not to Napoleon but to the exiled Snowball. The confessions and executions of the animals in *Animal Farm* are an allegory for the Moscow Trials of the 1930s, show trials for the benefit of the world at large, with elaborate and sometimes unbelievable confessions 'proving' the guilt of the accused and therefore justifying Stalin's actions.

The cult of personality, an almost religious attitude towards the Party's Leader, is allegorised by the hymns written to Napoleon and the near-worship of his person. We can see this attitude clearly in Boxer's motto 'Napoleon is always right'.

Stalin's wheelings and dealings with the West during the Second World War are allegorised by Napoleon's trading with the humans, and the selling of the timber to Frederick, who pays in counterfeit money and then attacks Animal Farm, represents the Nazi–Soviet non-aggression pact of 1939 and the invasion of Russia by Hitler, who was defeated at the Battle of Stalingrad in 1942. The conclusion of the story, where the farmers all meet and agree to work together, but eventually quarrel, allegorises the Teheran Conference where Roosevelt, Churchill and Stalin came to agreements as allies against the Nazis.

Throughout this story of animal rebellion against a tyrannical and exploitative leader and the rise of a new leader who perverts the principles on which the republic was built, ruthlessly pursuing power and personal ambition, we can see many analogies with the Russian Revolution and the rise of Stalin. The betrayal of the Russian people, which Orwell wanted to expose, is presented carefully through the betrayal of the animals by one of their own kind.

3 SUMMARIES AND CRITICAL COMMENTARIES

Chapter 1

Summary

The book opens with Mr Jones, the proprietor of Manor Farm, lurching across his yard and going off drunk to bed. The animals, waiting for his light to go out, assemble in the barn to hear what Old Major, the prize Middle White boar, has to say to them. We meet the animals on the farm as they arrive and already know something of their characters as they settle down to listen. Major has had a dream; he is approaching the end of his time and wishes to communicate to the others the wisdom he has acquired during his long, thoughtful life. This, briefly, is what he tells the animals:

(a) Animals' lives are 'miserable, laborious and short'; they live at subsistence level while working to capacity; the moment they cease to be useful they are cruelly killed; misery and slavery is the lot of all animals in England.

(b) The reason this is so is not that the land cannot support them but because the produce of their labour is stolen by man; remove man and the problem is solved.

(c) Man is the only creature that consumes without producing, taking everything from the animals except what is absolutely necessary to them.

(d) Animals are not allowed even to live out their natural span but are slaughtered when their function is fulfilled.

(e) Therefore animals must work night and day to overthrow man. In otherwords – Rebellion.

Major sums up by telling the animals that 'All men are enemies. All animals are comrades.' He then describes his dream of a world without man and teaches them the song that presents this dream-world. As they sing it Jones wakes up and shoots his gun, breaking up the meeting.

Allegory
Jones represents the capitalist class and the animals represent the people of Russia. Old Major represents both Marx and Lenin – Marx in his speech which is a summary of Marxist theory with echoes of the Communist manifesto, and Lenin in the way he brings the animals together – Old Major having them assemble physically in the barn suggesting Lenin's attempt to unify the Russian Marxists in their opposition to Tsarism. Both are represented in the call to revolution and the reclaiming of what is rightfully theirs. The song 'Beasts of England' closely resembles in parts the revolutionary song 'L'Internationale'.

Commentary
Right at the beginning of the book the tone is set with the drunken Jones neglecting to make sure his farm is safe for the night. Jones of Manor Farm, with its lord-of-the-manor connotations, is not managing affairs effectively but looking after only his own interests. He is quick enough to pick up his gun at the end of the chapter when he thinks a fox might be decimating his chickens.

As the animals assemble to listen to Old Major we are introduced to them in such a way that their natures are at once established and they are sympathetically presented on the whole so that Major's speech is the more shocking when referred back to these docile and decent-seeming creatures.

Major's speech is an effective piece of rhetoric and worth considering closely to see how it works. In one way it is typical of Orwellian rhetoric, a manner of expression he developed – striking a first blow for impact and then qualifying it later to adjust the balance of persuasive power with truth. In Major's speech the impact is felt with: 'It is summed up in a single word – Man. Man is the only enemy we have. Remove Man. . .and hunger and over-work is abolished for ever.' This is the impact blow, struck to make the listener sit up and take notice, the qualifying of the statement comes afterwards. The logical movement of the speech also carries us to its conclusion; accept each paragraph in turn – and they are constructed in such a way that they cannot be refuted – and the conclusion is indisputable. This main impact blow is also – in retrospect – bitterly ironic, for this was the ideal that is eventually betrayed.

While we were introduced to the animals as docile, even caring creatures before Major's speech in order to increase its effect, once it is over Orwell changes tack and the dogs' natural instincts are seen in their dive for the rats. Coming so immediately after the idealistic call to rebellion and the statement 'All animals are comrades' this seems to present a belief that revolution can never be successful – not because of mismanagement, bad luck or unforeseen circumstances but because of elements inherent in the nature of man. Orwell did come to believe, like Swift before him, that there was something wrong with human nature which prevented a permanent change for the better. Major's comment that the animals' lives are 'miserable, laborious and short' echoes the seventeenth-century philosopher Thomas Hobbes whose point of view – that life is 'nasty, brutish and short' – Swift appeared to uphold in *Gulliver's Travels*, Book IV.

Animalism is suggested by Old Major as a way of improving this life but does not suggest a compromise, only the removal of an enemy that exploits the animals and reduces them to a kind of slavery. Orwell does not seem to accept that this is all there is to it, suggesting that it is not only extrinsic elements that prevents things from improving. He seems to be suggesting that it is man's nature (animal nature in the story) that prevents any kind of Utopia from being achieved. The episode of the rats sows the seeds of this pessimistic philosophy.

It is not necessary, however, to be totally pessimistic, for the episode can be read to mean that human (or animal) nature must be taken into account, not just theories and ideas. Both these and the nature of those who pursue them must work together and the new life will be achieved only if these work together.

Chapter 2

Summary

Three days after his speech Old Major dies peacefully. His ideas have been taken up by the pigs – who are clever animals – and a political philosophy is worked out which is called Animalism. The other animals are not very interested and the pigs have a hard time trying to educate them, especially where the tales of Moses are concerned. Boxer and Clover are seen to be very loyal and supportive. The rebellion takes place almost accidentally because the animals are hungry and can stand it no longer – Jones has neglected them – so they break out and help themselves.

The animals eventually manage to evict Jones and his men from the farm and they joyfully discover that it is theirs. We find out that the pigs have taught themselves to read and write and Snowball changes the name on the gate to 'Animal Farm' and writes up on the barn the principles of Animalism – the Seven Commandments. The pigs have taken over as leaders quite naturally and Snowball urges them off to the hayfield to get in the harvest while Napoleon stands guard over the milk which the pigs have just milked from the cows.

Allegory

The 'secret activity' described in this chapter represents the educational programmes, the Marxist study groups, which were set up to educate the workers in Russia both in the basic principles of Marxism and more generally so that they would be able to take their places when the revolution came. Police records of 1901 describe as 'intelligents' young men with revolutionary tendencies.

The two pre-eminent pigs, Napoleon and Snowball, represent Stalin and Trotsky and their names are apt. Napoleon, who is to become dictator, is named after Napoleon Bonaparte who became Emperor of France after the French Revolution had run its course and reinforces Orwell's point of view that all revolutions are failures because out of them eventually rises a new dictator. Snowball is an apt name for the pig Snowball as he represents Trotsky who wanted to pursue world revolution or a 'snowball' effect in the move towards international socialism. It is apt too as he is slandered, or has his name blackened by Squealer, Napoleon's propaganda pig, who can turn 'black into white' and, by implication, white into black.

Animalism, of course, represents Communism, and the reactions of the animals – the apathy, the stupidity, the loyalty to the 'Master' (Tsar) echo the reactions of many of the Russian people. Mollie represents those who leant towards the west, and the ribbons and sugar suggest the luxuries that the 'decadent capitalists' indulged in at the expense of the workers, and the selfish desire for non-essential consumer goods.

Moses represents the Russian Orthodox Church – Marx had referred to religion as 'the opiate of the people', as another device of capitalism to sustain itself; Trotsky organised Societies of the Godless and these are alluded to in the pigs' struggle against the lies of Moses. Boxer and Clover represent the supportive element of the proletariat, those who wanted the Bolsheviks to seize power in their name and trusted them. Lenin's *April Theses* contained the slogans 'Peace, land and bread' and 'All power to the soviets', a rallying call at a time when the government was discredited by the failures of the Red Army, and desertion and hunger were rife.

In the fiction, rebellion comes before it is expected, almost for the same reasons – Jones had 'fallen on evil days' and his farm was going to rack and ruin, as Russia was being exhausted and demoralised by civil war. The assuming of leadership by the pigs is the seizing of power by the Bolshevik Party.

Commentary

It is necessary to the plot that Major's body is 'buried' but this seems strange while Jones is still in charge – he would surely have sent Old Major to be slaughtered. This is one of those instances where credibility is sacrificed to the schematic approach. Does it matter, the student should ask, do we even notice? If not, why not?

Notice the matter-of-fact narrative tone of paragraph 2 and the way the contrasting characters of Napoleon and Snowball are presented – only those qualities that are to be developed in the story are sketched in. With Squealer it is different. It is very important that we have a description that makes us see and hear him, for it is to be his physical presence, his mannerisms and expressions, that ultimately seem to be his greatest asset. He disarms the animals rather than parries with them.

The pigs are the 'clever' ones who can organise and teach, and in this chapter the antithetical, or contrasting, characters of Snowball and Napoleon are presented. Snowball is concerned with the ideological principles of Animalism and attempts to make Mollie see them too, eventually burning her ribbons when Jones has been expelled. It is Snowball who changes the name on the gate to Animal Farm and who paints up the Seven Commandments. It is also Snowball who urges the animals off to the hayfield to get in the harvest. Napoleon, we see, seems to be in charge of the rations, he gives out the corn and the biscuits and he stands over the milk while the others go off with Snowball to the hayfield. They have lived out in the chapter the comments that were made about their characters in the second paragraph – Snowball is shown to be inventive and lively while Napoleon is a taciturn presence that is felt rather than seen.

It is possible to view their partnership in this chapter as something that might work, each having something different to offer, or to see the differences that will eventually split them. It is often said that Napoleon's action in keeping the milk shows that he was from the very beginning concerned only with what he was going to get out of the new way of life, while Snowball was genuinely and constantly concerned only for the success of the new regime and the animals' welfare. Snowball, however, does not question the appropriation of the milk. The reader must make up his own mind.

The characters of Mollie and Boxer are brought out clearly in this chapter – again a strong contrast being made; Mollie is interested only in a comfortable life, in sugar and ribbons while Boxer accepts everything the pigs say. Their characters are presented in their attitude to Snowball's comments on clothes and their future behaviour predicted by their actions – Mollie does not want to part with her ribbons and eventually runs away in order to keep them while Boxer throws on the fire the straw hat that he used to keep off the flies in summer and eventually over-reacts again and again by working too hard and ruining his health.

It is in this kind of subtle and clever patterning that much of the delightful design of the fable can be appreciated. Another example of patterning is evident in this chapter – the list of instruments and paraphernalia used to keep the animals in bondage is contrasted with the later list of luxuries the pigs find in the farmhouse – artefacts of exploitation and privilege. The patterning is obvious also in the way they are listed, 'unbelievable luxury' and 'degrading' setting the tone for each list.

It is worth noticing how much is made of the animals' reaction to the rebellion rather than the action itself. Why has Orwell done this? Is it to demonstrate that the animals, once making a move, had together an almost irresistible strength, or that Jones and his men were cowards? Or is it to deflect the reader's attention to the result rather than the event? All the clues are in the episode and are worth looking for.

The writing up of the Seven Commandments should be a very serious event in the chapter – they are to contain the principles of Animalism, to direct the behaviour of the animals in their new way of life. But how is this episode presented and what is written up? There is considerable humour here – the picture of a pig up a ladder is comic enough and gets a comment in the narrative but the inaccurate spelling adds a touch of humour also – even the clever pigs are not perfect and make the most basic mistakes.

The Commandments themselves, we see, are not really principles at all but are based upon the most casual accident – the animals have just been in the farmhouse where they see clothes, beds and alcohol; they see men as their enemies and have destroyed the implements that prevented them from being equal. These Commandments are propaganda, slogans to appeal instantly to what the animals are feeling at this precise moment. Just as the rebellion happened by accident, the 'principles' are incidental. 'All animals are equal' is the basic reduction of Animalism but we have noted that Napoleon has taken charge of the milk and can make a guess about its destination; we can notice too the use of the word 'revealed' in the phrase 'the pigs now revealed that. . . they had taught themselves to read and write' which says a great deal. While this is not in itself sinister, it does prefigure the later deceptions and revelations.

Chapter 3

Summary
The animals have worked hard and the harvest is a great success. We hear how the different animals rate as workers and Boxer gets a special mention, doing the work of three horses. On Sundays there is no work but a ceremony where the flag is raised followed by meeting where resolutions are put forward and debated.

We hear that the pigs have set aside the harness room for a study and workshop area and that Snowball has formed many committees to educate the animals and encourage them in their efforts and attitude. We hear how the animals fare at reading and writing and that the principles of Animalism are reduced to a slogan 'four legs good, two legs bad' as many of the animals cannot read very well. Snowball, however, has developed his ideas into some complexity and uses long words the animals cannot understand. The puppies of Bluebell and Jessie are taken away by Napoleon to be educated, the milk and apples have been appropriated by the pigs and this is justified by Squealer and accepted by the animals.

Allegory
The difficulties that the animals find in running the farm could refer to the many difficulties that were encountered during the Cultural Revolution when workers were promoted to administrative jobs and began to flood into the elite category of 'leading cadres and specialists' – just as the pigs do.

Boxer is probably a representative of the Stakhanovite movement which encouraged workers to grossly exceed their quotas – the movement was named after a record-breaking coal miner. Unlike the Stakhanovites, however, Boxer is not resented by his fellow workers even though his personal motto is 'I will work harder', which he puts into practice. The statement that each animal worked according to his capacity refers to Marx's maxim 'From each according to his ability, to each according to his need.'

The hoof and horn on the flag represents the hammer and sickle (the communist symbol of unity between agricultural and industrial worker) while the Meeting where all the resolutions are put forward by the pigs represents the dictatorship, not of the proletariat, but of the Bolshevik party. Snowball's committees satirise Trotsky's Workers' Committees that he set up to educate the illiterate masses and teach the principles of Marxism. Snowball's simplification of the Seven Commandments into a slogan corresponds to the simplification of Marxist theory into slogans, and his explanation about wings and legs is a satire on the language of Marxism.

Squealer's approach at the end of the chapter is a parody of Stalin, who said in February 1931, 'In the past we had no Fatherland, nor could we have had one. But now that we have overthrown capitalism and power is in our hands, in the hands of the people, we have a Fatherland, and we must uphold its independence. Do you want our socialist Fatherland to be beaten and lose its independence?' This kind of statement is obviously satirised time and time again in Squealer's appeals to the animals.

Commentary
Because the farm is their own the animals work hard to make the harvest a success – every animal, with few exceptions, works according to his capacity and it is the combined effort that wins the day.

Or is it? While on the surface this is seen to be so, a close reading reveals that it is through the animals' eyes that we see this to be the case. The leadership of the pigs is taken for granted in the casual, 'it was natural that they should assume leadership' where the word 'assume' is very telling, as 'revealed' was in Chapter 2. The pigs do not actually do any physical work – contrast the verbs used to describe the pigs' activities: 'think', 'directed and supervised', 'walking' and 'calling' with the other animals' activities: 'toiled and sweated', 'use', 'mowing and raking', 'tramp', 'gathering', 'carrying', 'tread' and 'blow'. Both sets of activities are tied together with the phrase, 'but the pigs with their cleverness and Boxer with his tremendous muscles always pulled them through'. Here a contrast is made between the brain-power of the pigs and the muscle-power of Boxer, a balance that pulls the farm in the right direction, for the time being anyway.

Notice how necessary Boxer is; without him the farm would not have succeeded – to what extent is Orwell commenting that Napoleon rose to power assisted by Boxer? Is Boxer's loyalty and singlemindedness, later to be his downfall, a good thing or not? Does his volunteer labour and his motto suggest anything other than his desire for the farm to suceed without Jones? Would Benjamin's more balanced arrangement, 'never shirking nor volunteering for extra work either' have been more appropriate and less fatal in the end? Boxer is 'the admiration of everybody' and Benjamin is a cynic – what does Orwell mean to suggest by their behaviour here? If Boxer had not used up his strength and Benjamin had been less of an outsider, would things have been different?

When considering the themes of the book these contrasts between characters are important and are obviously intended as a comment upon human nature and those elements within it which affect the direction society takes.

After a description of the way the animals work we hear about Sunday when there is no work but the outcome of the revolution is implicit in the meetings where, we learn, 'it was always the pigs who put forward the resolutions' and hear that Snowball and Napoleon can never agree.

This chapter is structured very carefully and contrasts work very well. We have the contrast of the animals at work and at recreation and both are seen to be profitable to the success of the farm; then we have the contrast between physical work and mental activity, firstly in the getting in of the harvest where the pigs do the brain work and the others the physical work, and then in the contrast between the animals who excel at physical work but are very stupid when it comes to learning to read. Boxer, we see, is very good at one and no good at all at the other. The two descriptions relate to one another in a satisfying way as the contrast between the implements of exploitation and the artefacts of luxury did in the previous chapter. Benjamin, we see, holds the same position in both activities but he is the only one who is seen to do so and a contrast is again made between Boxer and Mollie, presenting Boxer's overzealousness and Mollie's concern only with decoration.

Another contrast is made between the lack of attainment on the part of the animals, who could get no further than the letter A when learning to read and are actually referred to as stupid, and Snowball's complexity of ideas and language. The animals need the Seven Commandments, simple enough in themselves, reduced even further to a slogan while Snowball distinguishes himself by his tortuous reasoning and long words. Notice the careful contrast of 'did not understand' with 'but they accepted' – a presentation of the trust that is to be betrayed – and 'words' with 'explanation', suggesting the possibility of distorting the truth which is later to be Squealer's speciality.

How does Orwell intend us to view Snowball? Is he worthy of the animals' trust or is there something in his nature that makes us wary? Squealer's 'explanation' about the milk and the apples coming shortly after this incident and immediately after a comment on their short memories certainly presents the animals' own natures as a threat to their future happiness.

Chapter 4

Summary
Some months have passed since the Rebellion and the news has spread to other farms, assisted by the pigeons sent out by Snowball and Napoleon. Jones is apparently making no effort to win back his farm and the neighbouring farmers are too involved in their disagreements to unite and help him. Pilkington and Frederick, Jones' erstwhile neighbours, laugh at the idea of a farm run by animals and spread tales about the terrible goings-on at Animal Farm, which they continue to call Manor Farm, but they are both frightened that their own animals might follow suit and flog any animal heard singing 'Beasts of England', which is becoming very popular. There are small rebellions on other farms but these do not amount to very much.

Jones, Frederick and Pilkington eventually do get together and make an attack on Animal Farm but thanks to the strategy of Snowball, they are repulsed at the Battle of the Cowshed. Snowball, Boxer and a dead sheep are decorated for their part in the battle.

Allegory
The spreading of the news about the rebellion, especially the use of pigeons to 'mingle' with the animals of other farms is probably a reference to the young Marxists who were sent out into the countryside to mingle with the peasants – the mushiks – to spread the word about Marxism and try to educate the peasants in its principles, or at least acquaint them with its ideas. This was basically a failure as any real

understanding of the peasants and their way of life did not occur. The stories of cannibalism and starvation refer to real rumours of this nature that were spread about at the time of the enforced collectivisation of the farms which did, in fact, result in a great famine.

The waves of rebellion which broke out on other farms also echoes historical events and the behaviour of Jones, Pilkington and Frederick is a comment on the behaviour of the Tsar and the West. Pilkington represents Churchill and Foxwood, England – note the way Foxwood is described; Frederick represents Hitler and Pinchfield, Germany. Their names are cleverly worked out and worth investigating. The Battle of the Cowshed represents the Counter-Revolution.

Commentary

We are beginning to have a feeling of time passing and it is worth noticing how Orwell deals with this structural aspect of the book. Chapter 1 set the scene for us and laid out the principles of Animalism and Chapter 2 continues with: 'Three nights later old Major died,' followed later by 'June came and the hay was almost ready'. The rebellion takes place on Midsummer's Eve and Chapter 3 takes up the story with 'How they toiled and sweated to get the hay in' and 'all through the summer the work of the farm went like clockwork'. Chapter 4 picks up the time thread again with: 'By the late summer the news. . .had spread'.

This method is used throughout the story, the time structure being strung along in the simplest way by references to what is going on in particular seasons. This serves not only the purpose of moving on the action but also gives a continuity that is in keeping with the setting – the farm moving, as farms do, in time-honoured seasonal cycles. It also presents time through the point of view of the animals – the names of months are occasionally mentioned but it is the change in the weather or activity that punctuates the story rather than artificial time structures.

While we expect to suspend our disbelief when reading this 'Fairy Story' there are times when our credulity is stretched to the limit – surely, we might have asked, Jones could have come back after the rebellion with other farmers and recaptured the farm? Chapter 4 tells us in a careful and quite acceptable way why this does not happen until October, some months after the Rebellion, and we have laid for us here one of the Napoleon's stepping stones to power. It is in part due to the defects of character obvious in the humans. Orwell, seen to be criticising the Soviet Union in this book, is also making an adverse comment on the behaviour of the West, a point which is often overlooked. In this explanation we find a comment on human nature, on those defects within it that assist opportunists in their rise to dictatorship. Napoleon is later to exploit these weaknesses.

An example of list patterning is again seen here in the description of the waves of rebellion and the spread of the song 'Beasts of England'. This latter is said to be 'irrepressible' and could be said to represent the human spirit which Napoleon is later to crush when he forbids the singing of the song, replacing it with another. This idea of song expressing the free spirit is found again in *Nineteen Eighty Four*.

Snowball's character is developed in this chapter. He has planned the Battle of the Cowshed in advance, expecting an attack from the humans and he leads the animals to victory, fighting bravely even when wounded. The animals obviously trust him and are prepared to follow his lead. However, it is obvious that he is a true revolutionary for he reproves Boxer for his sentimentality over the stable boy and emphasises the need to be ready to die for the farm. Snowball, seen to be working continually for the well-being of the farm and presenting an attractive personality is, nevertheless, not shown to best advantage against Boxer's moral goodness when he says 'the only good human being is a dead one'. We are happy for Boxer that the stable boy is only stunned for we admire his tender-heartedness.

Boxer and Mollie are again here contrasted, Boxer fighting bravely and exhibiting his great strength as well as his concern for the welfare of even the enemy boy he thinks he has killed, Mollie hiding away as soon as the battle begins and being concerned only about herself.

Where, we might ask, is Napoleon? What is the significance of his absence here? Do we assume he is among 'the rest of the pigs' and is not mentioned because this is Snowball's scene and it is the latter we are to associate absolutely with this Battle, seeing it from the animals' point of view? Or is Napoleon's absence indicative of some aspect of his character not yet developed? It was Snowball who led the animals off to bring in the harvest and Snowball again who leads the action here. Before the story develops further it would be as well to think about the significance of this. Another thinking point is the description of the action here, developed in some detail, which contrasts sharply with the brief account of the actual rebellion. Why has Orwell chosen to do this?

Notice how the fantastic and the authentic are again combined in this chapter, the animals' particular characteristics – the pigeons muting, the geese pecking, the sheep prodding and butting together with Muriel and Benjamin, while Boxer rears up on his hind legs – give authenticity to the presentation of the Battle. The fantastic ideas – the animals having celebrations and decorations, naming the battle and important dates in the history of the Rebellion – give a fairy-tale atmosphere but also an accurate imitation of human behaviour. The Battle of the Cowshed and its immediate aftermath is an example of the great charm Orwell gives his fable by combining the two.

Chapter 5

Summary
Mollie begins to act strangely here and Clover becomes concerned about her behaviour and takes her aside to tell her that she has seen Mollie's activities with the neighbouring farmer – Mollie has been allowing him to stroke her nose. Mollie denies this but Clover later finds sugar and ribbons in her stall. Eventually Mollie defects and is seen in Willingdon pulling a dogcart.

We hear that the pigs decide all policy matters connected with the farm and as these had to be backed up by a majority vote all might have been well for a while but for the disagreements between Napoleon and Snowball. Their main disagreement is over the windmill which Snowball wants to build to make the running of the farm easier and the life of the animals more comfortable. Napoleon maintains that the immediate concern is to produce more food.

Eventually two factions develop under the slogans 'Vote for Snowball and the three-day week' and 'Vote for Napoleon and the full manger'. They also have a major disagreement over the defence of the farm; Snowball believes that if the other farms have rebellions there would be no need to defend the farm so the best thing would be to send out pigeons and help these rebellions come about while Napoleon wants to get hold of firearms and be ready to defend the farm against an attack. When the issue is to be decided at the Sunday Meeting, the story reaches a climax. When Snowball gets up and passionately defends his ideas, the puppies Napoleon has educated bound in at a whimper from him and attack Snowball who is run off the farm and just manages to escape with his life.

Napoleon immediately rescinds all democratic running of the farm, cancelling the Sunday Meetings and telling the animals that the pigs would now be in control of all farm matters. There is some protesting but this is immediately quashed by the growling of the dogs. Squealer later goes round the farm to justify Napoleon's behaviour, stressing the importance of discipline. Eventually the animals hear that the windmill is to be built after all and that the plans were stolen from Napoleon by Snowball.

Allegory

Mollie's defection in this chapter probably represents those White Russians who defected to the West for a comfortable life no longer possible under the Bolsheviks in Russia. The decision that the pigs decide all policy refers to the Politburo. The disputes between Napoleon and Snowball represent the enmity between Stalin and Trotsky who were competing for leadership, and the building of the windmill represents the drive towards industrialisation.

The bitter difference of opinion and the slogans: 'Vote for Snowball and the three-day week' and 'Vote for Napoleon and the full manger' refer to one of Stalin's and Trotsky's most important differences – Trotsky wanting to give manufacturing priority over agriculture and Stalin wanting to collectivise the farms. The other important difference is over defence, or maintaining socialism. Trotsky supported world revolution or international socialism while Stalin supported socialism in one country and the building up of Russia into a great power.

Snowball's confrontation with the dogs and his expulsion from the farm represents Trotsky's exile – the dogs representing the GPU or secret police. Minimum represents the socialists artists and the writers of songs and poems praising Stalin. Under Stalin's conformity the arts languished, indeed, Lenin had written: 'Down with non-Party writers! Down with literary supermen! Literature must become a part of prole-tarian activities in general; it must become a "wheel and a screw" of the single great social-democratic machine which is driven by the whole conscious vanguard of the whole working class.'

The building of the windmill represents the first of the Five Year Plans. Although Stalin and Trotsky were in disagreement over indus-trialisation initially, Stalin later accelerated its tempo and his exactment of a 'tribute' or tax from the peasants is represented by Napoleon's warning that it might be necessary to reduce the animals' rations.

Commentary

This chapter is the turning point of the fable – the upward movement in the life of the animals has reached its peak and the downward move-ment is about to begin. Again, it seems that all the activity is Snowball's – he has been studying books and now makes use of his knowledge in plans for improvements; he has a vision of a future where machinery will take the drudgery out of life and he works towards this in a state of excitement; he wants to send out more pigeons to stir up the animals on other farms. In contrast, Napoleon 'produced no schemes of his own', he enlists the help of the sheep and he wants to procure firearms to defend the farm. He appears to be quietly planning in his own way – for what we do not know – but any movements he makes or plans fade into insignificance beside the feverish activity and innovative thinking of Snowball. When Napoleon does eventually make his move it is an effective climax for we have, with the animals, been full of admiration for Snowball and have been giving him our full attention. The careful reader will have noticed, however, the small events that have been leading up to the climax but it is usually only in retrospect that they are recalled. There has been the episode with the milk and apples, and the taking away of the puppies. In this chapter Mollie has defected and the winter has begun with earth like 'iron'. There have been disagreements between Snowball and Napoleon, carefully presented, graduating from the trivial to the serious.

This section of the chapter is worth close analysis as it is a good example of a narrative technique often employed by Orwell in the fable. The chapter does suggest an undercurrent. Napoleon, we are told, 'seemed to be biding his time' which contrasts strongly with the immediacy of Snowball's actions, his plans and projections. Snowball is open while Napoleon is, as yet, a closed book. When at last the day comes that Snowball's plans are finished and the vote is to be cast we see that Napoleon has been waiting only for the right moment, the time when Snowball is likely to supersede him as leader. Snowball is ousted. He has dominated the first section of the book, its upward movement, and is now displaced by Napoleon who rises throughout the remainder of the story to greater and greater power which corresponds to the downward movement in the quality of the animals' lives. 'Silent and terrified' they creep away and notice that the dogs wag their tails at Napoleon as they did at Mr Jones. This identification is made, then, as soon as Napoleon takes control and the conclusion becomes inevitable from this moment. We are reminded of Mr Jones and of the days of oppression the animals had thought gone forever only to realise that they will come again. Napoleon's ascendancy is represented by the 'raised portion of the floor' he stands on to make his announcement.

Look carefully at the contrasts of this chapter which make it a most effective narrative – the description of the chase of Snowball contrasting with the succeeding paragraph, the presentation of the characters and activities of Snowball and Napoleon, the use by Napoleon of sheep, and dogs which seemed like wolves – traditional opposites. Read carefully too the explanations of Squealer who 'was sent' to justify Napoleon's action, and his later explanation of Napoleon's change of mind about the windmill; 'he had seemed to oppose the windmill' the animals are told and this use of the verb 'seemed' sets the pattern and tone for an important aspect of the book, the use of confusion to manipulate. Fear as a coercive force is also introduced here and we can see that the outcome is all contained in embryo in this important chapter.

Chapter 6

Summary

We hear that the animals are working like slaves but are happy in their work because it is for themselves, not to support idle and wasteful human beings. We also hear that because of the building of the windmill, some tasks were left undone. The windmill is difficult to build as the animals are not well adapted for the tasks involved but they find a way round the difficulties, albeit a slow and laborious one. Boxer comes into the limelight again as his great strength is an asset and he puts his all into the work, so much so that Clover warns him about not overstraining himself.

Despite their efforts, the animals do not have the materials they require and this presents another difficulty. Napoleon decides to get round this by trading with the humans, something that upsets some of the animals as they remembered that initially it was decided never to have anything to do with humans, the enemy. Protesters are silenced by the growling of the dogs and Squealer tells them later that they must have been dreaming, that no such decision was ever made. The pigs into the farmhouse and sleep in the beds and again Squealer justifies this by altering the Commandment.

Animal Farm is beginning to be accepted by the humans, grudgingly, and they no longer support Jones who has, anyway, given up all hope of ever being reinstated. When the windmill is blown down by a November gale Napoleon blames Snowball and the animals believe him. They are deeply shocked that Snowball should do such a thing.

Allegory

The building of the windmill represents Stalin's first Five Year Plan, which was a failure. This plan was over-ambitious and there were serious difficulties such as lack of materials, skilled labour and transport, represented by the difficulties the animals have building the windmill. Failure to meet unreasonable targets and every failure within the plan was often treated as sabotage - just as Napoleon, not wanting to be responsible for the destruction of the windmill and being unwilling to admit that it was not strong enough to withstand the gale, blamed Snowball for its ruin.

The sacrifices the animals have to make in releasing hay, wheat and eggs for sale in order to buy materials they need represents the sacrifices the people of Russia had to make to fulfil the Five Year Plan. The manufacture of consumer goods, even essentials, took a back seat so that targets could be met. Eventually there were food and housing shortages. These shortages made it possible for Stalin to dispense privileges and 'closed shops' were opened selling goods that much of the population could not buy. These were often opened in priority areas where a particular target was being aimed at. These shops were also available to other privileged sections of the population and this is represented by the new luxuries enjoyed by the pigs. Stalin refused to admit that any sacrifices were being made, 'It is clear that the worker's living standards are rising all the time. Anyone who denies this is an enemy of Soviet power.'

This political use of the lie - with fear reinforcing it - is represented by Squealer's lies with the threat of the dogs behind them. We see in this chapter that Animal Farm is beginning to be accepted by the humans and this represents the acceptance of the Soviet Union by the West. It was expanding at a time when the West was in the middle of one of its greatest depressions and many western experts came to help with the Soviet Union's construction. This is represented here by Napoleon's decision to trade with humans.

Commentary

In the first paragraph we hear that the animals are happy to work so hard and for such long hours because they are working for themselves, not for someone who is exploiting them - the humans. This is, of course, ironic for they are working for a new exploiter although they don't yet know it. Orwell makes this point fairly soon afterwards by referring to 'strictly voluntary' work which, nevertheless, if not done will result in a fifty per cent ration reduction. This point is made again when one of the evils of working for humans is to be reintroduced - the giving up of the produce of labour for sale. The farm is moving towards what it once was – this is an important step in this direction and the animals are understandably uneasy. Fear is again used to quash protest and the usefulness of the sheep is noticed – they can cover awkward moments with their mindless slogan-chanting which has already been used to good effect to prevent discussion. Mr Whymper, the agent who is engaged to work on the farm's behalf, is presented as a crafty opportunist and we feel no good will come of him as far as the animals are concerned. Quite casually Orwell makes the point about Whymper being on two legs and Napoleon being on four – thus reconciling the animals – so that the difference between the animal and the enemy is still apparent and the slogan still holds good.

It is the gradual introduction of corrupt practice that is part of Napoleon's success, keeping the animals in a state of perplexity that can be, to some extent, assuaged by the assurances of Squealer. Just as soon as they have accommodated to some new action on the part of Napoleon and the pigs, another change is introduced and again justified.

It is worth exploring how this process takes place in this chapter and the reactions of the animals on each occasion. When trading is announced there is some uneasiness and a small protest which is quashed by the dogs and the sheep. Squealer does his job and the animals 'were satisfied that they had been mistaken.' When the pigs move into the farmhouse the animals again remember a resolution but Squealer 'was able to convince them'. Clover was not quite convinced and asked Muriel to read out the Commandment from the barn wall, but they find it does not say what they expected it to say. The matter is cleared up by Squealer who is passing with some dogs and 'no more was said' about the matter. When the pigs decide to get up an hour later in the morning, awarding themselves a further privilege, 'no complaint was made'.

Gradually the response of the animals is changing, they have become accustomed to mistrusting their own senses and memories and to accepting Squealer's justifications. They no longer dispute anything. The climax of this group of examples is the blaming of Snowball for the destruction of the windmill. Why do they not realise that Napoleon is lying, we may ask, for all the facts seem to prove it. The animals have seen what the wind has done to the flagstaff and to the elm tree and to accept that it was the wind that also destroyed the windmill seems to be nothing but common sense, and to think otherwise seems perverse.

They believe Napoleon, however, and here Orwell makes the very important point that often people will believe what they want to believe, that the credulity of people, their willingness to be deceived rather than face up to the truth, is a stepping stone for those who pursue power. All the animals are shocked, we are given to understand, and not one of them openly questions Napoleon's statement. It could be argued that they now no longer question anything, believing what they are told absolutely. This chapter presents the process by which they have been brought to this state of constant confusion and fear. The reader must make up his own mind.

Either way Napoleon uses his power to alter the past for no one will contradict him. As one aspect of politics that especially repelled Orwell – he was horrified that lies would pass into history – this was one of the motivating forces behind the writing of *Animal Farm*. In this chapter he presents this process and the way people can be hoodwinked and their way of seeing things determined. Truth is ceasing to exist on *Animal Farm* and the animals no longer believe the evidence of their own senses.

Chapter 7

Summary
It is a bitter winter and the animals' life is hard. They are often cold and hungry and have been depressed by the ruin of the windmill; they are not so hopeful as before but must succeed because the rest of the countryside is watching, ready to rejoice if they fail.

Food becomes very short and rations are reduced, the potatoes are spoiled and starvation seems a possibility, a fact they have to conceal from the outside world as new lies are being put about by human beings that famine and disease are rife and that cannibalism and infanticide are resorted to. Napoleon fills the food bins with sand and puts the grain and meal on top of it to hide the facts from Whymper, who is deceived. Eventually it is decided that the hens must give up their eggs so that they may be sold for grain and meal. The hens protest and smash their own eggs but Napoleon starves them into submission. He is advised by Whymper to sell off some timber and vacillates between selling it to Pilkington and Frederick who both want to buy it. In the spring Snowball is discovered to be coming into the farm at night and sabotaging the work of the animals. Napoleon decides an investigation should be made when it is discovered that Snowball has always been an agent of Jones and intends to attack the farm.

The animals do not believe him and Boxer, especially, speaks up on Snowball's behalf, reminding everyone of how he fought at the Battle of the Cowshed. Squealer, however, manages to carry the day but it is obvious he is displeased with Boxer. Four days later the dogs attack four pigs and Boxer too. Boxer fights them off but the pigs confess to have been plotting with Snowball and are killed. The hens who had started the egg rebellion are also killed. The animals are deeply shocked and creep away confused and miserable. When they comfort themselves by singing 'Beasts of England', Squealer arrives and tells them that this song is now outlawed and they must no longer sing it. A new song is composed which they sing at the Sunday meetings.

Allegory

The 'outside world' watching Animal Farm is the rest of the world watching the Soviet Union to see how things will turn out, and the rumours of infanticide and cannabilism represent stories that were being told about life in Russia at this time of accelerated industrialization and continued enforced collectivisation. It was a period of great hardship which resulted in a famine in which more than three million people are reputed to have died. Excessive requisitioning of grain ruined peasants and left them with nothing for themselves.

The hens' rebellion suggests the peasants' revolt against enforced collectivisation – they destroyed farm implements, killed their cattle and burned their crops. This, of course, contributed directly to the famine which followed. The reputed discovery that Snowball had always been an agent of Jones and was sabotaging the farm suggests the accusation that Trotsky was organising and directing industrial sabotage and terrorist attacks. It was put about that anything which went wrong was due to the activities of his supporters.

The confessions and executions represent the Great Terror, the Purge Trials, that period in Soviet history when oppositionists and Party members alike were eliminated on an enormous scale. Stalin got rid of everybody who did not support him absolutely and no one seemed safe; even the head of the secret police was arrested and executed together with most of his senior officials.

While those outside the Soviet Union were not aware of the scale of the terror, many foreigners wondered what made old, loyal revolutionaries confess to sabotage and the undermining of a way of life they had fought for so courageously. Was it torture and drugs? Their confessions were so incredible. The fear of the animals after the executions represents the terror that swept the Soviet Union, augmented by confusion and an inability to predict what would happen next. Akhmatova, the Russian poetess, wrote of this time:

The stars of death shone upon us
And innocent Russia writhed.

The work of the Russian novelist Alexander Solzhenitsyn presents the indiscriminate nature of arrest and exile and a reader interested in what it was like for many at the time would do well to read the short work *A Day in the Life of Ivan Denisovitch.*

Commentary
The beginning of this chapter is a good example of Orwell's control of the point of view. Squealer's work is succeeding for it is his point of view that is presented through the animals' eyes. Note the use of the verb 'knew' which is significant after the episodes in the previous chapter where Squealer has persuaded them that what they thought they knew was 'not the case'. To 'know' something now means that the animals have been *told* it is so, no more.

Things are beginning to go wrong on the farm, life is hard, the animals feel discouraged and food is becoming a serious problem. This again reminds us of life before the rebellion as the animals originally rebelled at such a time, and we make comparisons. Orwell has arranged his narrative so that we constantly look back and make these comparisons, and we are kept closely in touch with the feelings of the animals as well as directed towards a deeper understanding of the processes at work on the farm. This he does more than once in this chapter. When the hens decide to thwart Napoleon we are told 'for the first time since the expulsion of Jones there was something resembling a rebellion' and we begin to identify Napoleon more and more with Jones. It would be a useful exercise to look back over the past two chapters and see in what way this identification is being made.

One of the most important elements of this chapter is Napoleon's control of the past, its distortion and reconstruction, which was begun in Chapter 5 when Napoleon seized power. The first section of the book (Chapters 1-5) are forward-looking, it is to the future that our eyes, and the animals' eyes, are turned. There is optimism, hard work cheerfully done, plans and projections, everything with the vision of a life made easy and comfortable to raise the spirits.

But how is this happy time viewed once Napoleon is leader? In order to maintain power he has to alter the past. He needs a scapegoat for anything that goes wrong so that his leadership will not be called into question and he needs a way of getting rid of those who inconveniently refuse to believe what they know to be false. The animals can accept

Snowball as scapegoat for things that go wrong because this way they do not have to face up to the truth – that Animal Farm is not prospering as they thought it would, that things are beginning to go badly. This device helps to keep up morale.

However, when Squealer tries to convince them that Snowball has always been an agent of Jones they find this difficult to swallow and Boxer actually states his disbelief directly. Squealer's way of dealing with Boxer's reiteration of what actually happened is a good example of his skill in argument, his ability to turn white into black. He is successful, for most of the animals do begin to think they saw what he describes, and we remember that Napoleon did not figure directly in the battle Squealer is describing and this itself helps to give his acount credibility. At the critical moment, however, when Boxer refuses to swallow the story, Squealer turns on a different tack and confronts him with the words of Napoleon himself – a shrewd move, for to Boxer Napoleon is always right. In Squealer's 'ugly look at Boxer' lies Boxer's future, for he has shown himself to be inconveniently resistant to reconstructing the past as directed. When the dogs attack him we are not too surprised although the action amazes the animals who view him as their hero. When Squealer's speeches on the dignity of labour failed to move them, they found inspiration in Boxer's strength and resolution.

In the previous chapter we saw how lies were being used to control the animals and in this chapter we see that not only what the animals *thought* is to be distorted but also what they actually *saw*. The truth is what Napoleon says it is and the difficulties this will present are overcome by getting rid of any animal who refuses to accept it. The pigs who confess and are executed are those pigs who protested when the Sunday Meetings were abolished, and again when trading with humans was begun. The hens who confess are those who rebelled and smashed their eggs, Boxer had contradicted Squealer and Boxer is attacked, being saved only by his great strength and the fact that the windmill could not be built without him. It is when he is no longer useful that he is dispensed with – his loyalty to Napoleon makes him safe enough until such time.

An identification is made again between Napoleon and Mr Jones: 'Since Jones had left the farm, until today, no animal had killed any other animal', we are told, being reminded that in Jones' days there had been bloodshed enough. But now it is even more terrible, for Napoleon is one of themselves, not an enemy of animals as the humans are. As the animals creep away to the knoll from which they once viewed with pride the farm which had become their own after they had ousted Jones (Chapter 2), the main thrust of the story is clear – they have been betrayed. The great sadness of this realisation, of a revolution betrayed, of ideals debased, of a vision receding, is heightened effectively by the lyrical passage which begins, 'The animals huddled about Clover', who represents stolid virtues, common sense and human warmth and caring. Here disillusion is presented gently and convincingly and the true pathos of the animals' position is felt.

However, while we feel for the animals and realise the sadness in their disillusion, comforted perhaps that they still have spirits that are independent enough to recognise their loss and hearts still free enough to feel it, we are roused again to anger and left with a feeling almost of despair when Squealer arrives to announce that 'Beasts of England', that emotional song that has carried them through so much and that represents the spirit of the animals, is forbidden. Napoleon is going to crush even this. It is not enough that he controls their action and directs their thoughts, he is to become 'an engineer of the. . .soul'. Social realism is to replace idealism. In Orwell's work, song is used to represent the free spirit – especially in *Nineteen Eighty Four*. Here we see Napoleon is going to allow only what will serve his interests, songs that express what he wishes the animals to feel will replace those that express what they actually do feel.

Chapter 8

Summary
The chapter begins with another example of a commandment being adjusted and the animals' uneasiness about the matter is relieved. They assimilate the executions into their way of life. We hear that they now have to work very hard indeed, even harder than when Jones was in charge, and food is very short. However, as they can no longer remember these times very well Squealer has no difficulty in persuading them that they are wrong.

Napoleon is becoming a cult figure; he is absolute ruler and is given inflated titles which suggest his good leadership and general benevolence. He is praised for everything that goes well and has a hymn composed to him which is written up on the wall of the barn at the opposite end to the Commandments. He also has a young pig to taste his food in case it is poisoned. He begins complicated dealings with Pilkington and Frederick over the timber which they both wish to buy. Rumours of an attack by Frederick are heard and about the cruely he imposes on his own animals and feeling against him runs high. The windmill is eventually finished and is to be called Napoleon Mill.

Then Napoleon amazes the animals by telling them that he has sold his timber to Frederick and that all the rumours about him were the work of Snowball who has been on Pilkington's farm all the while. Napoleon pretended friendship with Pilkington to get Frederick to raise his price, they are told. However, the banknotes with which Frederick pays Napoleon are forgeries and he attacks the farm with guns and blows up the windmill. Eventually he is repulsed by the animals who suffer great losses in the Battle of the Windmill but Napoleon declares a victory and celebrations follow. The pigs discover whisky and get drunk, passing it off as illness, and Snowball is caught altering the Commandment but the animals are too stupid to realise what he is about.

Allegory
The affairs between Napoleon, Pilkington and Frederick represent the attempts by Stalin to play off the democracies against Hitler during the Second World War, eventually signing a pact with Germany. He had no reason to suppose that France or Britain would support the Soviet Union in an attack by Hitler but he also had impure motives for coming to terms with Germany. These were the possible expansion of the Soviet Union's boundaries by the seizing of part of Poland and the recovery of territories lost in the Revolution. However, this move contradicted all the official anti-Fascist policies of the Soviet Union and the communist media and created some confusion in the Party abroad. Many members left the Communist Party.

When the war began, however, communists abroad were instructed to criticise an imperialist war but it was suggested that Britain and France were more to blame than Germany. Anti-Fascist news was suppressed and Nazi atrocities were not to be mentioned. Stalin's mistake was that he would not believe the rumours of impending conflict with Hitler – he who told so many lies was himself deceived. Everything had to be mobilised to defend Russia when the surprise attack by Germany took place and after many disasters the people responded to patriotic appeals, as the animals do despite their growing disillusion with their way of life. Industries in the Soviet Union had to be moved from threatened areas and a great disruption of industry was the result – represented by the blowing up of the windmill. Eventually the Germans were defeated at the Battle of Stalingrad, which is represented in the satire by the Battle of the Windmill. Napoleon's announcement of a great victory represents Stalin's position after defeating the Germans.

Commentary

The chapter opens with a further adjustment to the Commandments to justify actions that have been forbidden. Once again the animals are satisfied but this now irritates the reader. After the pathos of the animals' position at the close of the previous chapter (the horrors they have witnessed and the disillusion they have suffered), we expect something more of them but they accept that there was 'good reason' for executing the traitors and are satisfied.

The admiration we felt for Boxer when he was so upset about the stable boy, the enemy he thought he had killed, can be brought to mind here to contrast with this rather glib acceptance of mass murder. Have the animals been corrupted morally by Napoleon, we must ask, so that they no longer recognise evil when they see it? While we may have found their easy acceptance of Squealer's persuasive justifications amusing or ridiculous throughout the book, there does come a time – and for many this is it – when the dark side of their gullibility becomes almost culpable. Thought-control is Napoleon's crime but the animals are not entirely innocent either and if we have not seen it before we now realise that this is one of Orwell's intentions. Look at these animals being duped, he is saying in the fable, are you sure that you yourself are not being duped? And if you are, shouldn't you be doing something about it? This becomes one of the moral imperatives of the fable.

The character of Benjamin should also be looked at in closer detail. He has kept well out of things; he did not believe in the revolution, nor in the hope that life would improve in any way. Here he refuses, as usual, to go and read the Commandment. How culpable is Benjamin? Is Orwell asking us to look at people like him and question their policy of letting well alone? Is Benjamin's crime one of omission? He has brains – why does he not use them to guide his comrades until it is too late? Or is Benjamin rather like Orwell himself, disillusioned by revolutions and promises of Utopia, wiser by experience and not interested in the machinations of yet another aspiring tyrant? It is worth looking carefully at his character. In this chapter he looks on in wry amusement while Frederick and his men get ready to blow up the windmill – only he knows what is going on. Is this an occasion for 'amusement' or is there no other course left for Benjamin? When what we call human values are at stake, he acts quite differently; he is devoted to Boxer and with Clover exhorts him not to overwork. He is finally roused to action only when Boxer is being taken away.

As a fable demands that all the participants are looked at closely because – like the pieces on a chess board – they each have a part in the winning or losing of the game, we must consider the actions of all the animals. Napoleon's obvious crime, Squealer's particularly disgusting role, the animals' gullibility – and perhaps Benjamin's laissez-faire, his tendency to let well alone – all contribute to the conclusion of the story.

We should be asking ourselves what defects of character in the animals collectively are together maintaining Napoleon's position? How did he manage to get supreme power? Are the animals collectively presenting those human characteristics that Orwell saw as preventing the affairs of men from improving?

The adulation of Napoleon as a cult figure is an important feature of this chapter and it is with some reservations, surely, we accept that the inflated, ridiculous poem composed by Minimus expresses 'the general feeling on the farm'. Do the animals really admire Napoleon so much; are they really that stupid? Any reservations we have are dispelled when they swallow Squealer's nonsense about Snowball. The series of reconstructions about his part in the Battle of the Cowshed are worth looking at again to show the process by which they can come to believe, eventually, that Snowball ran into the battle with the words 'Long live humanity' on his lips (Chapter 9). We could say that Napoleon gets his deserts when, after cunningly prevaricating with Pilkington and Frederick, he is paid for his timber in false notes and Frederick attacks him, but it is the animals who suffer.

Greed, Orwell has been showing us throughout this fable, is one of the major ills of society – it not only means that some privileged few have more than their share, leaving others short, but its results can be unexpected and catastrophic. 'Then we have won back what we had before,' Boxer tells Squealer. Consider this statement carefully in relation to what we, ourselves, might regard as victories. Consider also why this battle was far more ferocious than the Battle of the Cowshed.

The animals were fighting for their farm, they thought. In reality they were fighting for Napoleon, urged on by an appeal to their patriotism. Napoleon is here using what is commendable in them to maintain his own invidious position. It is worth referring to Karl Marx's statements on the use of nationalism to support capitalist wars to appreciate fully the extent of Orwell's irony here, but the technique is, of course, of more universal application. It is one of our many ways of getting people to do what we want.

Chapter 9

Summary
Boxer is growing old and his wounds from the battle heal slowly. Clover and Benjamin exhort him not to overwork himself but he continues with the rebuilding of the windmill. He will soon be of retiring age and we hear that there is a rumour that a new place will soon be designated for retired animals now that the original field has been used to grow barley.

Life on the farm is getting harder and harder and rations are reduced. Squealer, with his figures, argues to the contrary or presents the facts in a distorted way. The animals are always ready to believe, as usual, that things are not so bad as they were before the rebellion. Their morale is kept up by the 'Spontaneous Demonstrations' that Napoleon arranges and by the tales of Moses who has been allowed back on the farm by the pigs.

Boxer works so hard that he strains himself and falls ill. His popularity is shown by the fact that half the farmyard rush to where he lies. Squealer says that it has been decided to send him to hospital and a van arrives one day to take him away. Benjamin rushes out to tell the animals and he also tells them what is written on the van. They are sending Boxer to the knacker's. They shout to Boxer and try to rouse him to break out of the van but Boxer has no strength left to save himself. The pigs deny this has happened and explain the mistaken rumours by saying that the van changed hands and the name of the Horse Slaughterer was not yet painted out when the vet took over the use of the van. The pigs promise to hold a memorial feast for Boxer but instead they drink a case of whisky which has obviously been bought from the sale of him to the Horse Slaughterer.

Allegory
In this chapter the manipulation of figures by Squealer again represents the insistence by Stalin that the standard of living was rising all the time – figures were constantly being produced to prove this. The growing gap between the pigs' way of life and that of the animals represents the growing hierarchical structure of soviet life.

Boxer's death probably represents the death or exile of so many ordinary people during the Terror – many were taken off to concentration camps. The van Boxer is taken away in also suggests the gas vans of

Hitler. The return of Moses to the farm represents Stalin's attempt to reconcile the church, an attempt which brought him world-wide contempt and ridicule. The use of language to pervert the truth is satirised here in Squealer's substitution of 'readjustment' for 'reduction'.

Commentary

It is worth looking carefully at the structure of this chapter. It opens with a paragraph on Boxer – we hear that his wounds are taking a long time to heal and that he is still working hard. Then we hear about the hopes the animals have generally about plans for retirement when they are too old. Immediately afterwards we hear that Boxer's twelfth birthday is not far away.

In these two opening paragraphs we have been prepared for the end of Boxer's working life and wonder what will be in store for him. The following five paragraphs deflect our attention from Boxer to the machinations and hypocrisy of the pigs. We have been well prepared for the collapse of Boxer – we know he is no longer strong and is looking forward to his retirement and we have just been reminded of the extent of the pigs' hypocrisy and selfishness.

These two sides of the issue are waiting to be pulled together into the climax. The trust of Boxer and the concern of Clover and Benjamin are sown early in the chapter and are later developed to heighten the pathos of the episode and the hypocrisy of the pigs has been treated in the same way, being eventually developed into the totally absurd statement that Squealer makes about the name on the van. The final horrible bringing together of the two strands is that instead of a memorial banquet for Boxer which they promised, the pigs get drunk on whisky they purchased by selling him to his death. Look at other chapters in the same way and discover how Orwell has made them work effectively by carefully structuring events and developments, making parallels and pulling strands together.

We see in this chapter how the pigs take great pains to create the illusion that life is so much better than it was when Jones owned the farm, but we see also that life has become so hard that it is necessary to arrange ways to keep up morale. In this chapter manipulation of the animals is complete, they believe everything they are told, they are even 'glad to believe'. Orwell's irony should be closely studied here. It would be a good idea to go through the book collecting examples to analyse and decide in what way the irony changes in nature as the story progresses.

At the beginning of the story when we as readers know something the animals do not – for example, we are well aware of what will become of the milk in Chapter 2 whereas the animals are puzzled – we are amused, the irony has a comic side, we smile even though we sense in this the gullibility of the animals and its possible consequences. Now we are amused no longer, the irony has darkened and the moral aspect has asserted itself to the extent that the humour is overshadowed. There is nothing at all comic in the animals' acceptance of Squealer's statement about the name of the horse slaughterer's van. Trace the way that the nature of the irony has developed from that early example to this later one. *Try to analyse your response to the examples you pick out and the way that Orwell has controlled this response.*

Napoleon becomes dictator absolutely here, for his position is now officially recognised – there is only one candidate for the Presidency of the newly proclaimed Republic. All opposition has been physically or psychologically removed and the animals, who have just been ironically described as no longer slaves, are less free now than they were in Jones' day when they could at least believe the evidence of their senses and form their own concept of the world they lived in. When the animals are 'enormously relieved' to hear what Napoleon has to tell them and their sorrow is to some extent assuaged by the thought of Boxer's happy death, we are reminded of the swift way they accommodated to the confessions and executions – because they wanted to! This is a very important point that Orwell is making. We looked previously at the way it was the collective behaviour of the animals that helped to sustain Napoleon in power and caused the corruption of the ideals once held.

Again we do not feel that the animals have once more been deceived by the lies of the pigs so much as feel they are to blame for being so ready to be deceived. This episode has worked very much in the same way as the previous one – our sympathy has been engaged for a while and then, when we have identified with the animals and are outraged and sad for them, Orwell disconcerts us by presenting their worst qualities and disengages our sympathies to some extent. Look closely at how this is done in both episodes and compare them.

Now that Napoleon is acclaimed as sole leader and has removed every kind of opposition it would be worth while to trace by what methods he has achieved this and how the gradual identification with Jones – to be the climax of the next chapter – has been developed.

Chapter 10

Summary
Years pass until there is no one left on the farm who remembers when it was owned by Jones – except Clover, Benjamin, Moses and some of the pigs. We hear that no animal has ever retired. The farm has become prosperous and been enlarged, and the windmill has been built. It is not used to improve the life of the animals, however, but to mill corn for profit. Napoleon has said that luxuries, such as Snowball intended to supply with his windmill, were contrary to the spirit of animalism. The pigs and dogs have increased in number and consume a large proportion of the farm's prosperity without producing anything. They are too busy with essential paperwork, Squealer tells the animals. Despite a very hard life the animals feel privileged to belong to Animal Farm for it is still the only farm in England owned and run by animals. There are still celebrations which make the animals feel proud.

One day Squealer takes away the sheep to teach them a new song and on their return Squealer is seen walking on his hind legs. Napoleon follows, also upright and with a whip in his hands. Immediately the sheep begin to bleat, 'Four legs good, two legs better!' Clover has noticed some change on the wall of the barn and Benjamin consents to read what is written for her. He reads, 'All animals are equal but some animals are more equal than others.' This justifies all the existing privileges and all the new ones that the pigs give themselves.

Napoleon has a delegation of farmers visit the farm and he entertains them in the farmhouse. The animals creep up to look in the window. Napoleon is now on equal terms with the farmers and they make jokes about lower orders and lower animals which amuses them very much. Napoleon states that 'Comrade' will no longer be used and that the name of the farm will be changed back to Manor Farm. A quarrel breaks out when it is discovered that someone is cheating at cards. As the animals look from pig to human and from human to pig they notice that something has happened to the faces of the pigs – they cannot tell the difference between them and the humans.

Allegory
Here we see that the ideals of the revolution are betrayed absolutely. The neat maxim 'All animals are equal' which represented the socialist ideal has been corrupted and an established hierarchy is not only in effect but is officially recognised. The pigs' position represents the 'administered privilege' – Party-state officialdom controlling what is

produced and who gets it. Everything now works towards maintaining the status quo, keeping things just as they are – the revolutionaries have become conservative, conserving and maintaining their position of privilege and celebrating every victory that has assisted them on their way towards this. This was the situation that Stalin brought about.

Orwell satirises the huge bureaucratic machine in the 'files, reports, minutes and memoranda' which are written only to be burnt – this activity being necessary, Squealer says, to the running of the farm. The meeting between Napoleon, Pilkington and other farmers who drink a toast to Animal Farm represents the Teheran Conference at which Orwell believed Churchill, Roosevelt and Stalin planned eventually to divide up the world among themselves as three world powers – a situation he develops in *Nineteen Eighty Four*. The quarrel that breaks out when Napoleon and Pilkington play an ace of spades simultaneously could represent the beginning of the Cold War, the resumption of East/West hostilities after Stalin established party dictatorship in Czechoslovakia and Hungary in 1948.

Commentary
There is a change of time-scale in this last chapter. Previously, time has passed in a continuous flow, season upon season. How many years have passed since the opening of the story and the close of Chapter 9? It would be a good idea to trace this passage of time, note how it has been managed and decide how effective this management has been. Refer back to the commentary on Chapter 4 for some idea of how to go about this.

In Chapter 10, years have passed: 'the seasons came and went, the short animal lives fled by'. Time for Napoleon is an ally, for as it has passed he has gained greater and greater control and reconstructed the past to make of it an ally too. We hear that the animals lives are hard – they are hungry, cold, and troubled by flies in summer. Nothing much has changed for them and anyway there is nothing to which they can compare it. Orwell has brought his story full circle in this chapter in as many small ways as the more obvious ones. The animals' lives are 'short' he reminds us and nothing but work. Benjamin tells us that hunger, hardship and disappointment are 'the unalterable laws of life'. If we refer back to Old Major's speech before the Rebellion we will find that he referred to life then as 'miserable, laborious and short' and the Commandments which were written up by Snowball after the Rebellion were to be 'the unalterable law by which all the animals on Animal

Farm must live for ever after'. Orwell has carefully chosen his words to give his conclusion the greatest possible impact. Find other examples of this careful attention to detail in the chapter.

It would seem that the unalterable law of life is the only thing that has not changed for the animals with the passage of time. Those ideals they clung to, where are they? We see that these too have been perverted – into pride for Napoleon's regime. The Commandments have been corrupted as easily as they were invented and serve their purpose as well now as they did at the beginning. Were the Commandments ever accepted by all the animals as a true and unalterable law? Read again Chapter 2 and decide whether they were or whether they were merely slogans of the moment which outgrew their usefulness.

Consider the change in the sheeps' slogan. 'Better' now replaces 'bad'. What is the significance of this? Perhaps Orwell is reinforcing the point of view he presents through Benjamin, that there is no difference, finally, whatever the system and its ideology. Consider the impact of having Squealer seen first upon two legs, rather than Napoleon. Consider, too, why it no longer seems to be comic as it did earlier, when Snowball was standing on his hind legs up the ladder with Squealer below him holding the paint pot; the implications are now quite different and the pigs' aping of human activity has a sinister side to it that was not there before. Many details that we might have taken no notice of when we first read them, now fit into the pattern and together reinforce the irony.

It is interesting to notice how similar the animals' response to Napoleon on hind legs and with a whip in his trotter, is to their response after the confessions and executions – they huddle together in their fear but here the tension is relieved, not by the singing of 'Beasts of England,' but by the sheep with their new slogan; not by an assertion of the comradeship of animals, but by an acceptance of humans as superior beings to be emulated. We are being prepared here for the conclusion of the fable, Orwell preparing the ground carefully as he always does so that we are led to the response he wishes to produce.

When Napoleon and Pilkington begin to quarrel because one of them has been cheating, we are reminded of the double-dealing of Frederick and what the consequences to the farm were. Consider carefully what your final response is at the conclusion of the story. Is it anger, or sadness, or a combination of both? Is there a feeling of a truth having been told and a sense of aesthetic satisfaction, perhaps, at such a well-turned story? Think about your response carefully and how Orwell has brought this about, controlling the events, the point of view and the tone of the narrative to lead you where he wants you to go. At the close of the fable you should be able to appreciate how well purpose and style have been blended, that fusion of 'artistic purpose and political purpose into one whole'.

4 WHAT THE WORK
IS ABOUT

Animal Farm is a multi-level work. As the section 'The Choice of a Form' makes clear, these levels can be combed out to be looked at separately, and each strand would probably bring to the forefront a different theme or issue to be considered. It is firstly a fairy story, or a humorous tale about animals which can be enjoyed for its own sake, but the fable form is not far behind this reading of the story and we find that its moral is that 'hunger, hardship and disappointment' are an unalterable law of life, that principle gives way to expediency and personal ambition and the pursuit of power are tendencies of human nature that prevent amelioration from taking place. As Benjamin says, nothing ever really changes. *Animal Farm* can be read as an exposition of the pursuit of power, of the ruthless and cynical exploitation of one group in society by another, or of the whole of a society by an individual. Orwell seems to be suggesting that those who effect revolutions are, perhaps, too unscrupulous to rule justly, and the work comes down strongly against all revolutions, finding them unsatisfactory methods of effecting any real change for the better. *Animal Farm* can be read as a satire on revolutions generally and on the Russian Revolution in particular. Orwell has used allegory to clarify his satire and keep it close to actual events, but he did not have to do this. He could have written an effective satire on Russian Communism without using allegory, but the fact that he did so should not confine us to reading it as a satire of one particular system. We are obviously intended to read the work in a wider context and Orwell's own experiences of revolution are behind the writing of the book, the events of the Spanish Civil War as much as those of Russian history.

Animal Farm teaches us to be wary, to be awake to the reality of all kinds of dictatorship that threaten the freedom of the individual. Orwell himself said in a letter that it was 'intended as a satire on dictatorship in general'. When the Russian events he satirised have faded into the past, the purpose of his work will still be relevant: *Animal Farm* will continue to be read as a warning against the process of revolution and its aftermath. Orwell's intention, to get his readers to think about the future of Western society, and especially about the place of socialism within it, is as relevant today as it was in 1945 and, we can assume, will be so for a long time yet.

4.1 DEMOCRATIC SOCIALISM AND TOTALITARIANISM

There are, basically, two types of socialism, *revolutionary socialism* (the kind that was behind the Russian Revolution) and *evolutionary* or *democratic socialism*. The latter is concerned about the most efficient allocation of resources and to give the worker back the 'full product of his labour', insisting on full employment, social security and the redistribution of wealth through taxation. This should come about not through revolution but by constitutional means. *Totalitarianism* is a form of government which seeks to control all major aspects of social activity with total power and no opposition. In his satire Orwell presents his dismay at what he saw was being perpetrated in the name of socialism, at the 'swindle' being effected on the Russian people and at the debasement and corruption of principles for the sake of power and expediency. It is very important for the reader to understand clearly that it is totalitarianism in all its disguises that Orwell is criticising and democratic socialism that he vigorously defends at all times. *Animal Farm* is sometimes used as propaganda, as a plank in the arguments of those who oppose socialism. This is a distortion of its purpose.

Orwell no longer believed in Utopia, he no longer – after his experiences in the Spanish Civil War – believed in revolutions and he was concerned that socialism was being corrupted by a variety of influences. What he wanted to see was a revival of the original concept as he saw it, of justice and liberty. His purpose was positive and constructive in this work, not pessimistic and destructive as is often argued. True, he wanted to destroy a myth but this was because he felt it was the only way that a socialist revival could come about. The dangerous acceptance of everything the Soviet Union did, as the one country which had thrown off an almost medieval oppression and successfully taken its own affairs into its hands for the benefit of its people, was an acceptance based on lies and hypocrisies, Orwell felt. The picture of Russia under Stalin was a complete misconception brought about by a conspiracy of silence and by that tendency of man not to see what he does not want to see or to call it something other than what it really is. A reading of his essay 'Inside the Whale' will give the reader some understanding of how he viewed the growth of the Communist movement in England, its admiration of Russia and the reason why so many western communists did not criticise any of the inconsistencies that seem to us now so blatantly obvious.

Orwell's dismay was not only directed towards socialism in the Soviet Union. His criticism of home-grown elements that he considered counter-productive helps us to keep his work in perspective – he was afraid that many right-thinking people would be frightened away by much of what seemed to represent the movement. As he said in *The Road to Wigan Pier*, 'Socialism calls up a picture of vegetarians with wilting beards, of Bolshevik commissars (half gangsters, half gramophone), of earnest ladies in sandals, shock-headed Marxists chewing polysyllables, escaped Quakers, birth control fanatics and Labour Party backstairs crawlers' – a picture of the movement hardly likely to appeal to anybody of ordinary common sense and sound principles. His criticism, which he often published in *Tribune*, upset many of his readers. The view of him as a disillusioned socialist who became more and more reactionary as he got older is quite without justification. It was his dismay at what passed as socialism that provoked his criticism.

Life in England during the Thirties bred, he thought, a 'sort of Boy Scout atmosphere of bare knees and community singing'. It was so totally removed from 'violence' and 'illegality' of any sort that the dangers were not recognised – 'If you have grown up in that sort of atmosphere it is not at all easy to imagine what a despotic regime is like.' It was when the English did come to imagine what despotism was like – with the rise of Hitler – but failed to see it in the Soviet Union behind the then friendly face of an ally, that Orwell knew he could wait no longer to speak out.

To keep *Animal Farm* in perspective we must bear in mind Orwell's attitude to all 'smelly little orthodoxies', his hatred of all despotism, all kinds of tyranny. *Burmese Days* is as much a criticism of imperialism and the British Empire in India as *Animal Farm* is a criticism of what passed as socialism in the Soviet Union – both are examples of injustice –

and the body of work contained in his essays pleads for honesty in politics, an eye steady and clear that could look at something long enough to see what it really was, a tongue free from justifications when what was seen was not what was expected.

The Stalinist regime was not only unjust to the Russian people, Orwell felt, but was debasing socialism elsewhere. What was really significant was not what was happening but the way what was known produced no results at all in those who called themselves socialists. In the essay 'The Prevention of Literature' written a year after *Animal Farm* he says, 'The argument that to tell the truth would be 'inopportune' or would 'play into the hands of' somebody or other is felt to be unanswerable, and few people are bothered by the prospect of the lies which they condone getting out of the newspapers and into the history books.' His purpose was not just to present and expose the lies but to separate out the corrupt form of socialism from the true one. If this type of socialism produced the same effect as other forms of dictatorships – and Orwell makes quite clear in *Animal Farm* that he thought it did – then people ought to know about it and recognise what had happened. This would be a warning and perhaps alert people to the processes that had been taking place.

It has often been said that if *Animal Farm* was written to alert the public to social and political injustice then it came too late, that it was not a prophetic warning but merely an exposition of an event that had already taken place. Reading *Animal Farm* leads us to ask: if a deception of this kind could take place in these circumstances and in this way, in what other circumstances and ways could a similar effect be produced? If *Animal Farm* is looked at only as a warning against allowing the Soviet model of totalitarianism house room in our society what dangers do we leave ourselves open to?

In 'Why I Write' Orwell states, 'Every line of serious work that I have written since 1936 has been written. . *against* totalitarianism and *for* democratic socialism, as I understand it.' It is all manifestations of totalitarianism that we should be on the alert against, not allowing ourselves to be lulled into the false security of thinking that we know where it is and what it looks like, arming ourselves against it. This satire suggests that the processes by which it arrives are often disguised and unexpected.

4.2 A REVOLUTION GONE WRONG

In *Animal Farm* Orwell presents his disillusion with two revolutions –

the Russian Revolution of 1917 and the Spanish Civil War in the Thirties. He had first-hand experience of the latter himself and it was his personal experience of the cynical betrayal of ideals in this war that is as much behind *Animal Farm* as his analysis and understanding of the Russian Revolution. He saw a system based not upon justice and liberty – his concept of what true socialism was about – but the exact opposite, injustice and oppression.

Animal Farm may have behind it these particular revolutions but it is an allegory of all revolutions which Orwell felt were always betrayed by the lust for power. Napoleon does not represent only Stalin but a type, and every revolution, Orwell suggests, breeds and nurtures this dangerous species. Illegality and violence that bring about a revolution also prevent the realisation of the revolutionary ideal – the process of revolution itself is not purifying but corrupting; it is not just an opportunity to overthrow an unjust law but gives power to the lawless. It is perhaps an occasion of necessary violence but it gives power to the violent. *Animal Farm* invites us to ask: can revolution's effect on a society be a permanent change for the better – does revolution bring about the *moral* change that is necessary for this?

It is the nature of revolution itself that Orwell wants us to look at, to beware of, if we are looking for a way of improving the human condition. *Animal Farm* is as much about human nature as the nature of revolutions and we might ask: do those qualities that make a successful revolutionary leader ever go hand in hand with humanitarian principles? Are those who effect violent change perhaps unfitted to be the ones who hold power afterwards? What safeguards are there to prevent such people from fulfilling only personal ambitions? All these questions are there – in negative form – in *Animal Farm*.

If we study the character of Snowball carefully we can see that he too could have become a Napoleon. However beneficial his schemes and plans may have been eventually (assuming they were practicable) he did belong to and condone the privileged class. Studying the book carefully we find no moral force behind Snowball's action as we do, for example, with Boxer's but we find plenty of evidence to suggest that as a rival for leadership he too, was ambitious on his own account. The episode in the chapter where he throws Mollie's ribbons on to the fire may suggest moral strength but it only breeds the kind of zeal that leads Boxer eventually to his death. Boxer's first over-enthusiastic action was, remember, to throw on the fire after the ribbons the straw hat that he used in the summer to keep off the flies. Would Snowball's kind of leadership have been as despotic as Napoleon's but in a different way? It is often argued that Snowball was concerned only with the animals' welfare, with improving their hard condition of life, but this is not the case. A close reading reveals that it is the plans and ideas and the theories that Snowball is most concerned with.

Animal Farm suggests that revolution is not the answer to the problems of 'hunger, hardship and disappointment', that even different types of revolutionary leadership have a common root – personal ambition or the desire for power in one form or another. Orwell believed that Lenin, had he lived longer, would eventually have become a dictator and that the Russian people would have fared no better had Trotsky won the bid for leadership instead of Stalin. Orwell's naming of Napoleon after the French Emperor Bonaparte may well be a way of suggesting that a revolution in the name of the people, of liberty and justice, always results, eventually, in the rise of an opportunist who can exploit the new political situation for his own ends.

4.3 PESSIMISM OR REALISM?

In *Animal Farm* Orwell suggests that one of the unalterable laws of life is 'hunger, hardship, and disappointment'. He presents this law at the beginning of his fable when Jones is boss and he presents it again at the end when Napoleon is boss. If this is the case, we might argue, then what is the point of the fable? Has Orwell written it merely to depress us, to tell us that anything else is illusory and we might as well just accept it? This would not be a warning at all but merely an appeal to stoicism or cynicism. He is warning us that because this is so we must not follow illusions, we must not jump on bandwagons, blindly optimistic that this or that new set of ideas will change everything. We are warned against revolutions that promise Utopia, against believing that an ideal world can be attained. Here are different human characteristics – greed (pigs), intelligence (pigs), vanity (Mollie), lazy opportunism (the cat), the easily led (sheep), blind loyalty (Boxer), co-operation and hard work (Boxer and others), deceit and hypocrisy (pigs), warmth and caring (Clover), cynicism (Benjamin), etc., etc. When you think that some new system might change society, look at these, his fable warns, and remember that ideas have to be tested in action, that in practice it is individuals upon whom results depend, individuals with characteristics such as these. The perfect cannot be built with the imperfect.

The fable makes us look at human nature and find it wanting. If we cannot change our nature – and it seems that Orwell is pessimistic on this point – then we must avoid situations where the worst of human failings may flourish and do the greatest damage. We must organise things so that greed and self-interest and intelligence are not set against blind loyalty and gullibility. We must 'play the game' differently so that the Napoleons of this world do not always win; hunger, hardship and disappointment may not be altogether avoidable but the degree to which they are present in society depends upon how we manage our affairs, accepting them as a law of life maybe but ameliorating them as far as possible. This is not pessimism, but realism. This is not a lack of faith in human nature but a realistic acceptance of it in all its variety. Orwell always had great faith in the 'decency' of the common man. 'Old-fashioned' virtues, unselfishness and a caring attitude must be at work to minimise the effects of man's perennial pull towards self-interest, towards the pursuit of power. It is an acceptance of human nature and a skilful combination of human virtues and failings that will ameliorate the hard laws of life, Orwell is suggesting, not ideas that cannot accommodate what man is.

5 TECHNICAL FEATURES

5.1 STRUCTURE

When we look at the structure of *Animal Farm* – the architecture of the book, the skeleton around which the details are built – there are three aspects we can consider: there is the *time structure* of the story, the *narrative structure* and the *ironic structure*.

Time structure
The *time structure* is simply presented and easily followed. We move from 'early in March' (Chapter 2) through the rebellion which takes place in June, on Midsummer's Eve (to give it extra impact) and into the harvest of Chapter 3 which takes us 'all through the summer' to the late summer of Chapter 4 when we hear that news of the rebellion has spread. In October the Battle of the Cowshed takes place and in Chapter 5 we are in winter and Mollie disappears. It is a hard winter through January and Snowball is busy with his plans and eventually chased off the farm. Chapter 6 compresses time with 'all that year' and 'throughout the spring and summer' into 'as summer wore on' and the pigs move into the farmhouse. Autumn and November also pass and in the latter the windmill is destroyed in a south-westerly gale. The winter that begins Chapter 7 is again a bitter one with snow and cold and hunger and in the spring there is the Snowball scare, the confessions and executions – at the same time of year that Old Major had made his speech in the barn. Time is again compressed in Chapter 8 with 'throughout that year' and 'summer wore on' into the autumn when the Battle of the Windmill takes place and the windmill is again destroyed, about a year after it had been destroyed the first time by the storm. In Chapter 9

we are again in a cold winter with food shortages, continuing through February when the comforting smell of what might have been a warm mash turns out to be beer being brewed for the pigs. In April of this year the farm is declared a republic and the fourth year begins. In the summer, Moses returns and Boxer's health fails and he is taken away. Chapter 10 breaks this rather tight but naturally-flowing time-sequence with 'Years passed. The seasons came and went, the short animal lives fled by.' This last chapter moves us on over many years to a time when most of the animals who were alive when Jones was in charge have died and even Boxer is almost forgotten except by Benjamin and Clover, both now old. This time structure has followed the seasonal changes and the seasonal farm activity in a way most appropriate to the rural background of the story, the occasional compressions of time contributing to the fairy-tale quality. At the close of a traditional fairy tale there is often a change in time structure but here it is used ironically to contradict the usual 'and they lived happily ever after'.

Narrative structure
Upon the time structure of the story is constructed the narrative structure, the events that take place. It is at this structure that much criticism of the story is levelled. When Orwell is criticised for over-simplifying, for failing to bring out the complexities of an event or following through a logical sequence, he is misunderstood. This telescoping of what could be difficulties in the narrative, what could break the spell of enchantment if pursued, stretching our credulity too far for comfort, is part of the ironic structure of the book and is also a feature of the fable form. This compression, this method by which the narrative is limited, has a purpose – to focus the reader's attention on particular patterns within the narrative so that an ironic point is brought home.

Ironic structure
The broad ironic structure of the book is contained in the upward movement that takes place until Chapter 5 when Snowball is chased from the farm. From this time the movement gradually descends through the confessions and executions to the death of Boxer and the final twist of the conclusion, the irony darkening from the early, humorous, light-hearted, more comic tone. Within this broad structure there is a complexity of internal patterns which creates the ironic design of the book. Many of these have been discussed in the Chapter commentaries. A look at paragraph 4 of the commentary on Chapter 1 will remind you

of what to look for and how these ironic patterns work. You should look carefully at each chapter in a similar way.

Interaction of structures

We must look too at the way the time structure, the narrative structure and the ironic structure interact: Old Major states the principles of Animalism at the end of winter or early in the spring – a time of hope and the emergence of new life – and it is at the same time the following year that Snowball is expelled from the farm. So much for 'All animals are comrades'! At the same time a year later the confessions and executions take place and in the spring of the following year, the close of the third year, the farm is declared a Republic – an event which is savagely ironic by now, this irony being reinforced by the cumulative effect of the interaction of time and narrative structure. Look carefully for all examples of this kind, for it is upon them that the satire is made effective.

While the plot is seemingly managed in a very straightforward way, a close reading will reveal the complexity of design that has, in fact, dictated the narrative structure. Events have been carefully selected and juxtaposed for maximum effect as the internal structuring of chapters show. The supporting timbers of the plot are those events which lead to the altering of the Seven Commandments and the ever-changing perspective on Snowball. Can you locate and trace these?

In the section 'The Choice of a Form' some of the characteristics of the fairy tale are discussed. At the close of a fairy tale a change in time sequence is often used to symbolise or present a change in form – often a change from an unenlightened childish form to an enlightened, or awakened one. Often a change from an animal form into a human form is presented, perhaps an enchanted person being restored to his rightful human shape. Are both these traditional conclusions used ironically in *Animal Farm*? The animal shape is what is here desirable and the human shape what is undesirable – the opposite of the traditional fairy tale conclusion. The animals are enlightened perhaps, but only when it is too late. (Does this enlightenment, if it is one, represent in *Animal Farm* political awareness?) Perhaps the conclusion is more positive. Perhaps there is hope that now the animals see the pigs for what they really are, there will at some time in the future be another rebellion, another bid for freedom. The reader must decide how to interpret the conclusion after a careful reading.

5.2 IRONY

Irony in *Animal Farm* is one of the means by which the reader is made to see what the author wants to point out, one of the means by which a relationship is built up between the author and the reader. Simply, irony is about contrasts and comparisons, about bringing together two aspects of an event so that we recognise contradictions or anomalies and become aware of what is happening in a special way – we have an insight that other characters in the narrative do not have. When something in a narrative *seems* to be the case and we, because we have been given a privileged view of the event, know it is not the case, irony is at work. The fable constantly invites us to be aware of contradictions, it uses design to put together two events so that we compare them, it spotlights for us things that the animals are in the dark about.

There are different types of irony and they should be identified as the reader traces examples through the narrative. Sometimes it is comic and sometimes it is quite savage. The sadness we feel on occasions – when the animals are huddled together on the knoll after the executions; when Boxer is taken away to the knacker's and cannot kick his way out of the van – is evoked by the pathetic quality of the irony while the sense of injustice we feel is evoked by the moral quality. To take the example of Boxer's departure – here we can see different types of irony operating at the same time: we are sad because Boxer has been presented sympathetically and this end is not deserved at all; we are outraged that Napoleon has done this when Boxer has always been loyal and hardworking; we are both sad and angry at the thought that had Boxer not used up all his strength working hard he might have been able to save himself; but how do we feel when Squealer justifies Boxer's departure with his lies? It is what we expect of Squealer but how do we feel about the animals' acceptance of his exaplanation? The irony becomes very complicated as the narrative develops and the response is similarly complex.

Early on in the story we were entertained by the humorous quality of the irony as much of what happened was comic and we tended to think the animals rather stupid for being so gullible. One of the features of the fable is the way the irony changes in quality, darkening as the story progresses. The easiest way to trace this change is to look at examples of irony in chronological order and ask yourself what your response is. When, for example, does your response to the altering of the Seven Commandments cease to be a wry smile at the cunning of the pigs and become one of outrage? Perhaps this change in response has already taken place before any of the commandments have been altered? A reader must decide for himself. To understand how the irony works in the fable it is necessary to study it carefully chapter by chapter, noting your response. When individual examples have been considered the ironic structure will take shape, as the effect of individual examples being added begins to form the pattern. Notice how the satire is presented through the changing nature of the irony – the humorous, the light-hearted, gradually giving way to the satiric.

5.3 CHARACTERISATION

As discussed briefly in the section 'The Choice of a Form' the fable does not present characters as such but *figures* or *representatives*, types which work closely within the ironic structure to present the *issues* that Orwell wishes us to notice. We do not expect to find here complex personalities or to be looking for change and development in the 'characters'. What we are looking for is the *function* of the figures, their particular role in the fable. The figures are constant, what they are at the beginning of the fable they are at its end, and while we may not have discovered early on what in fact this is – and we are not always intended to do so, of course – we do not have to adapt to change and development. The figures invite us to ask what they represent and how their movements effect the ironic structure and therefore the satire. The figures gradually reveal more and more of the same tendencies rather than variety and complexity of personality so that their role in the fable becomes more and more apparent as more and more of the same tendency is revealed.

When we study the characters of **Napoleon** and **Snowball**, for example, we see that this is so. We find in the early chapter that we do not know very much about Napoleon but we learn a great deal about Snowball. We should be asking ourselves why this is so. It soon becomes obvious that the first reason is that the early, or upward-moving, part of the book is Snowball's section – he is in his element and appears to be thriving until eventually he is in the position of potential leadership over his rival Napoleon; while in the second or downward-moving section of the book, Napoleon's section, it is the latter who gains ascendancy but only after Snowball has been ousted. As Napoleon rises, we see that it is by slandering Snowball and exploiting the animals' quite natural fear of invasion and the return of Jones. It is essential, we can then see, that we know a great deal about Snowball and not too much about Napoleon for the irony of this reversal to be effective. The animals are confused by Squealer's blackening of the former hero's character, but we as readers are not. They are made to doubt their memories, we remember very clearly all we learned of Snowball in the early section of the book and know what Napoleon is about. In this way Orwell achieves his ironic purpose. In the same way, as we know so little about Napoleon, the irony of the sudden reversal at the very moment when Snowball appears to have invented a system by which their life is to be made easier, is also made effective. We will have picked up one or two clues if we have been reading carefully – he was 'biding his time', we were told, and this turns out to be true. We are not as surprised as the animals are when he turns nasty and begins his rule of terror, for we have noticed the sinister elements of his character. These have not been many but they have been sufficient to warn us and they have been reinforced by the openness and liveliness of Snowball.

These two pigs' characters form one of the contrasts upon which the structure of the fable is built. The way they rise and fall, and the constant involvement, one with the other, is achieved throughout the narrative, is well worth exploring. Snowball is good at organising, at planning. He is intelligent and his objective is to educate the animals so that they are able to help in the governing of the farm. Napoleon is taciturn, he keeps his ideas to himself and works underground (as he does in taking away the puppies to train), while Snowball always works in the open. He is not mentioned in the Battle of the Cowshed where Snowball is fighting so bravely after working out the strategy by which it is won. Snowball wins support by his ability to arouse enthusiasm and support while Napoleon has, ultimately, to resort to force, evicting Snowball with his dogs when Snowball has won the day for himself in the dispute about the windmill. We can say that Snowball tends to be progressive while Napoleon is wanting to conserve his position and consolidate it. As the story develops after the expulsion of Snowball, the character of Napoleon is presented more openly to signify the position Napoleon now finds himself in. He does not have to hide his real nature now there can be no opposition. What opposition he meets he deals with in a most ruthless way. We can see, in retrospect, that the confessions and executions are present in the taking away and training of the puppies; at that point in the story Orwell keeps his motives hidden so that the reversal of upward-movement will be a surprise and therefore effective. In terms of strategy it was also, of course, essential for Napoleon to keep his thoughts, plans and intentions to himself. Napoleon is so utterly corrupt with no motive other than his desire for power that Orwell's theme – that power corrupts – is presented without the hindrance of a complex character, as an issue rather than a combination of motive and result. We do not need to question *why* Napoleon acted as he did. In the fable he represents ruthlessness, violence, betrayal, self-interest – those elements in revolution that Orwell saw working against the original intention. In this way the political intention, that power corrupts, is realised.

Boxer is the animal that most readers remember best along with Napoleon and he forms another of the important character contrasts with Napoleon that are vital to the ironic structure of the fable. The way we view Boxer is essential to the way we view Napoleon and he is presented sympathetically, and very simply, to reinforce our hated of all that Napoleon represents. Through Boxer we come to see Napoleon as a ruthless, exploitative, power-hungry creature and we loathe him for the way he treats Boxer. The fact that Boxer himself cannot loathe Napoleon because he is duped by him throughout the story – indeed, Boxer's trusting nature and his abhorrence of violence reinforces the process – makes us loathe Napoleon more. We hate Napoleon not only *because of* Boxer, but *for* Boxer. Boxer is presented as one of the most devoted of Napoleon's followers, never doubting for more than a moment what the Leader says any more than he would shirk his workload, imposing upon himself standards of achievement far above what is expected. Boxer represents those who believe that more of the same thing will bring the desired result when the present amount is failing, rather than consider that a course of action might be wrong. When things are going badly on the farm Boxer is determined to work harder – 'I will work harder' being one of his mottoes – believing that in this way affairs will improve. He also believes absolutely in Napoleon, even when this conflicts with what he thinks himself. It is Boxer's presentation as a simple, sincere and compassionate creature that causes the reader to be outraged, angry, and sometimes deeply grieved about the way he is treated, and his contrast in character with Napoleon makes us weigh up one against the other. A value-judgement is the result. We find a balance of opposites: Napoleon is ruthlessly cruel (the confessions and executions – Boxer's death) while Boxer is compassionate (the stable boy in the Battle of the Cowshed); Napoleon is all powerful in his cunning while Boxer is quite helpless in his trust and loyalty;

Napoleon is motivated by self-interest while Boxer is motivated only by a desire to do his best for all. Many more contrasts could be listed. We can see quite clearly Orwell's intention in his characterisation of this hard-working, devoted and betrayed horse.

Old Major is, of course, vital to the ironic structure and, therefore, to the satire. We meet him for the first and last time in Chapter 1, but his presence is felt throughout the fable. He is a thinker, he wants to pass on to the animals what he has thought out, that they have a common enemy – man. Only rebellion will free them, is his message. His function in the fable is as the instigator of the rebellion and the hinge of the ironic structure of the book. He is respected and the reader is straight away guided towards this response to him, 'he was still a majestic-looking pig with a wise and benevolent appearance'. It is essential we view him with respect for most of what happens afterwards can be referred back to him, one way or another. Old Major introduces the ideals that are to be systematically corrupted throughout the narrative. When the pigs are referred to in Chapter 2 as the cleverest animals, for example, we associate them with Old Major which is, of course, an intentional irony. His skull survives, is venerated, just as the bones of his ideas survive, refleshed by the pigs. His 'all animals are equal', which became one of the Seven Commandments, becomes 'but some animals are more equal than others'. It is worth looking at all the rewritten Seven Commandments and referring these and every corruption back to Old Major's speech. The pigs' corrupted version of his ideals is supported by Napoleon's travesty of leadership – Old Major having provided an example of benevolent leadership enabling us to make comparisons and then a value-judgement.

Each of the 'characters' in the fable can be looked at in this way, the reader discovering first what they represent in human terms, deciding their function from this, and then giving consideration to their place in the complete picture which leads us to consider the issues Orwell is concerned with. The section 'Summaries and Critical Commentaries' considers, chapter by chapter, this aspect of the narrative. The questions we may ask about Old Major's place in the fable could be these: why is he brought on at the beginning of the story instead of, say, in Chapter 2? Why do we learn about his character and ideas before any of the others? What is the effect of this in relation to the rest of the narrative? The reader should consider all the figures of the fable in this way, asking similar questions, relating the figures to one another and the structure of the narrative. The characters in this work are a part of the structure rather than a separate element working alongside it.

5.4 STYLE

Style is closely related to purpose and especially so in this narrative which was intended as a deliberate fusion of political and artistic purpose. In 'Why I Write' Orwell listed political purpose as one of the motives of a writer and describes it as, 'a desire to push the world in a certain direction, to alter other people's ideas of the kind of society they should strive after.' In 'Politics and the English Language' he says, 'In our time it is broadly true that political writing is bad writing' and this is partly so because it is 'the defence of the indefensible' and consists largely of 'euphemism, question-begging and sheer cloudy vagueness'. It is these that are so obviously absent from *Animal Farm*, euphemism being replaced by the simple and straightforward, question-begging by a clear presentation of events that speak for themselves, and vagueness by strong, effective prose. *Animal Farm* is an embodiment of Orwell's statement that 'Good prose is like a window pane'. The narrative directs us towards the issues he so urgently wanted to present and he demonstrates humorously in 'Politics and the English Language' that an urgent wish to communicate cannot be reconciled with an inflated or obscure method of presentation. A writing style, he is saying, reflects the sincerity of the writer and Orwell's style reflects his own sincerity of principle and purpose, never using effects (figures of speech, technical devices) for embellishment but only to push home the point he wishes to make. His *use* of language is married to its *purpose*, there is no ornamentation. In 'Politics and the English Language' he offers the following rules:

(a)   Never use a metaphor, simile or other figure of speech which you are used to seeing in print.
(b)   Never use a long word where a short one will do.
(c)   If it is possible to cut out a word, always cut it out.
(d)   Never use the passive where you can use the active.
(e)   Never use a foreign phrase, a scientific word or a jargon word if you can think of an everyday English equivalent.
(f)   Break any of these rules sooner than say anything outright barbarous.

In the same essay Orwell states: 'Political language. . .is designed to make lies sound truthful and murder resepectable, and to give an appearance of solidity to pure wind.' How does this statement sum up much of the language used by the pigs in *Animal Farm*? Where in

Animal Farm does he satirise jargon and 'pure wind'? For some guide-lines in studying the language of *Animal Farm*, refer to the chapter commentaries – especially Chapter 1 where the use of rhetoric is discussed and Chapter 3 where his use of verbs is looked at carefully. The reader should consider the language chapter by chapter to comb out various aspects – rhetoric, aptness of verb, simplicity of phrase, appropriate use of cliche, etc., etc. before looking at language in the broader terms discussed above.

The following section 'Examination of a Specimen Passage' has been chosen to demonstrate, among other things, Orwell's use of 'window pane' language, and this example, together with the discussion of language in the commentaries should enable a reader to appreciate this aspect of the narrative.

6 SPECIMEN PASSAGE AND COMMENTARY

6.1 SPECIMEN PASSAGE

The passage chosen for discussion consists of the first three paragraphs of Chapter 6.

All that year the animals worked like slaves. But they were happy in their work; they grudged no effort or sacrifice, well aware that everything that they did was for the benefit of themselves and those of their kind who would come after them, and not for a pack of idle, thieving human beings.

Throughout the spring and summer they worked a sixty-hour week, and in August Napoleon announced that there would be work on Sunday afternoons as well. This work was strictly voluntary, but any animal who absented himself from it would have his rations reduced by half. Even so, it was found necessary to leave certain tasks undone. The harvest was a little less successful than in the previous year, and two fields which should have been sown with roots in the early summer were not sown because the ploughing had not been completed early enough. It was possible to foresee that the coming winter would be a hard one.

The windmill presented unexpected difficulties. There was a good quarry of limestone on the farm, and plenty of sand and cement had been found in one of the outhouses, so that all the materials for building were at hand. But the problem the animals could not at first solve was how to break up the stones into pieces of suitable size. There seemed no way of doing this except with picks and crowbars, which no animal could use, because no animal could stand on his hind legs. Only after weeks of vain effort did the right idea occur to somebody – namely, to utilize the force of gravity. Huge boulders, far too big to be used as they were, were lying all over the bed of the quarry. The animals lashed ropes round these, and then together, cows, horses, sheep, any animal that could lay hold of the rope – even the pigs sometimes joined in at critical moments – they dragged them with desperate slowness up the slope to the top of the quarry, where they were toppled over the edge, to shatter to pieces below. Transporting the stone when it was once broken was comparatively simple. The horses dragged it off in cartloads, the sheep dragged single blocks, even Muriel and Benjamin yoked themselves into an old governess-cart and did their share. By late summer a sufficient store of stone had accumulated, and then the building began, under the superintendence of the pigs.'

6.2 COMMENTARY

This passage opens the chapter, the first chapter with Napoleon as Leader. We know that democracy is a thing of the past and the Sunday morning meetings have been abolished, a committee of pigs being set up to decide all policy matters. Snowball has been expelled and we await the new developments. We begin the chapter in some apprehension, despite Squealer's justifications, for we now view things differently; the distance between our view of things and the animals' view of things has widened and the nature of the satire has changed. Our suspicions about Napoleon have been justified. This first paragraph is a new beginning, a change of direction – the downward movement of the narrative begins here and we feel the difference in the irony of the opening paragraph. When we hear that the animals are happy despite their hard work because 'everything that they did was for the benefit of themselves. . . and not for a pack of idle, thieving human beings' we feel the pathos of their situation – the irony is darkening. We know now what the implications are of the animals' credulity, of their ability to accept so easily Squealer's lies and accommodate Napoleon's behaviour. The reference to humans here also makes us look forward, as well as back – is Napoleon becoming like a human, we are invited to ask, for the word 'slaves' has been chosen carefully, although its common usage in the phrase 'worked like slaves' lets it slide in unobtrusively and hides the irony. The reference to humans also reinforces the principle that all humans are enemies so that it is fresh in our minds when we come to hear that Napoleon is engaging in trade with the farmers and that Whymper is to visit the farm every Monday. Both the humans who are to come and the pigs (to whom 'idle' and 'thieving' could, perhaps, already be applied) are ironically present in the last phrase of the paragraph. This paragraph is a pivot, we look backwards and it leads us forward – both directions are ironically present.

Paragraph 2 begins to describe what is meant by 'worked like slaves' and so follows logically from the first. We hear that a sixty-hour week is worked and that Sunday afternoons – once the time for leisure and education – are now worked as well. There is no need now for the animals to be re-educated or to join societies. These were Snowball's ideas and they have now gone along with Snowball as the need to know anything except that 'Napoleon is always right' has gone too. At one time the animals worked each according to his capacity and we realise why this has been rephrased as 'worked like slaves'. The perversion of language – and of the concepts behind the language – is also neatly presented here. The work is 'voluntary' but we find that, in effect, the animals have no choice. If they do not 'choose' to work they will starve. 'Voluntary' has ceased to mean anything. The seeds of later hardships are also sown – the harvest was not so good as before, and even then rations were only just sufficient and there had been talk of reducing them; two fields have been left fallow as there was not time to sow them. Again the paragraph is a pivot which makes us look back and then turns us round to look forward; we feel a change of direction is taking place and that things are going to get worse – not better. This is a direct contrast to Chapters 1–6 where, despite hardship and some confusion, the direction was carried forward by the presence and optimistic activity of Snowball. The presentiments we felt at his exile are here intensified.

Paragraph 3 continues the logical structure of the paragraphing by presenting not the facts of their hard work but the actual nature of it. We have been moving in towards this detail from an outside position; the camera has been moving closer. We are able to visualise the animals at work, having to overcome specified difficulties – they heave huge boulders up the slope and let them crash down and shatter. Although we see this activity, the style is formal so that we see it as an onlooker, not as a participant; this paragraph does not let us feel the laborious nature of the work – the following paragraph does this, again a logical movement always nearer to the animals' experience. This paragraph presents the difficulties for us to see as a problem, rather than an experience; notice the abstract style of 'The windmill presented unexpected difficulties' and 'namely, to utilise the force of gravity'. Further examples of this formality are evident in 'a sufficient store of stone had accumulated' and 'under the superintendence of the pigs' which continues the experience of this paragraph as an onlooker watching the solutions to problems being worked out rather and feeling physical activity. This is typical of Orwell's style in *Animal Farm*, the language being exactly adapted to what it is to represent – here a problem, or problems, have to be solved and the language does this without distracting us in any way from its primary intention. This is precisely what Orwell meant by 'window pane' language. The magnitude of the problem is presented by 'even the pigs sometimes joined in at critical moments'. When physical effort is suggested as in 'they dragged them with desperate slowness' it can be seen that while the rhythm of the sentence suggests its meaning, it is still the problem of getting them to the top, not the activity in itself, that is getting our attention. The language here is simple, clear and effective, controlling our point of view and, being outside looking in, we can compare this problem-solving with the same activity in humans. The formal style, rather like reportage in places, contributes to this comparison. This 'reporting' style reminds one of *Gulliver's Travels* where formal language often presents absurd activity, and we realise that such activity is ridiculous when performed by animals. The paragraph, then, lightens for us what is to the animals a very serious business which again distances us from them. We are reminded of Snowball up the ladder and Squealer several rungs lower holding the paint pot. 'No animal could stand on his hind legs' is therefore seen to be an inaccuracy rather like the burying of Old Major (which would have been unlikely before the rebellion, because he would surely have been slaughtered), but we are not too disconcerted by this. It is, of course, an ironic statement looking forward to the time when, for lesser reasons than these, the pigs acquire this skill.

This passage is then an example of the way Orwell structures his chapters, moving us in paragraph by paragraph but at the same time turning us round to look over our shoulders so the ironic structure of the fable is gradually built up. It is also an example of the clarity and precision of his style which exactly presents its meaning without adornment. The irony is changing and one of the major ironic themes of the fable is presented. The animals are, in fact, working for a new exploiter but they don't know it and the reader is now well aware of both Napoleon's intentions and the possible fate of the animals. The opening paragraph lays the foundations for the 'Republic' that is to be sardonically alluded to in Chapter 9.

7 CRITICAL RECEPTION

Animal Farm was published in 1945 and its first printing of 4500 copies was sold out in two weeks. The reviews were all glowing and its favourable reception was in direct contrast to the difficulties Orwell had in getting it published. It has, basically, been seen in four ways – as a 'lighthearted tale' (Christopher Hollis, 1956), 'a cry of despair' (Stephen Greenblatt, 1965), 'a clever satire on the betrayal of the Russian Revolution and the rise of Stalin' (Stephen Greenblatt, 1956), and 'a backward work' (Isaac Rosenfeld, 1946) or a fable that 'misses the point' (Northrop Frye, 1946).

Many of the earliest critics were attracted to the way *Animal Farm* was written, to the humour, the wit, the tone of the work. Graham Greene in the *Evening Standard* of August 1945 comments on the 'humour. . .the subdued lyrical quality' but sees it essentially as a sad fable. Edmund Wilson in the *New Yorker* (1946) comments on the 'simplicity. . .wit. . .dryness' of the work and compares it with the work of the great satirists Voltaire and Jonathan Swift, viewing the tone as essential to the tradition of satirical animal fables. Some critics view the tone of the fable as the mood of the author, not as a means of controlling the response of the reader. Laurence Brander, in *George Orwell* (1954) sees it as a tale in which 'the gaiety in his nature had completely taken charge' a point of view he shares with Hollis, the book being viewed as a temporary respite from Orwell's more characteristic work. Hollis's *A Study of George Orwell* (1956) also sees Orwell's love of animals as one of the elements behind the charm of this work, disassociating the human representations from a charming presentation of animals that combines the realistic with the humorously fantastic. This view of *Animal Farm* as a 'gay and light-hearted message' is at odds with the more brutal elements – the executions, Boxer's death – and, indeed, with the purpose of the fable itself.

Richard Hoggart in *Introduction to The Road to Wigan Pier* (1965) refers to Orwell as 'the conscience of his generation' praising his 'passionate concern'. 'All of us may not be able to accept all his moral solutions', he says, 'but we are bound to respect his moral stance' and he includes *Animal Farm* in this appraisal. He reminds us that it is easy to be carried away by the direct, honest approach of Orwell and refers to the rage behind the writing of *Animal Farm*, a rage based on Orwell's 'continuing fierce suspicion of the emergence of a beehive state', a caution, perhaps, after an analysis of Orwell's polemic and sometimes 'intemperately violent' attacks. He sees *The Road to Wigan Pier* as 'fantastically inadequate' as an attack on socialists and this criticism is carried to some extent over to *Animal Farm* but with the rider that this attack on 'machine society' is controlled through 'apparently lighthearted allegory', which disappears again in *Nineteen Eighty Four*. What Hoggart calls 'passionate concern' in 1965, Greenblatt had viewed as 'a cry of despair' in *Three Modern Satirists* (1963), totally disagreeing with such critics as Brander and Hollis. He also contradicts the view that Orwell's love of animals is of any importance, 'Orwell in *Animal Farm* loves animals only as much or as little as he loves human beings.' He also disagrees with Hollis's view that a fable has to have a lighthearted message if it is to be successful. It is the dark side of the fable he uncovers, the work of a man who 'experienced daily the disintegration of the beliefs of a lifetime, who watched in horror while his entire life work was robbed of meaning'.

Greenblatt also refers to *Animal Farm* as 'interpreted most frequently as a clever satire on the betrayal of the Russian Revolution and the rise of Stalin' and this is evident in the earliest reviews. Graham Greene (1945) sees it as 'a welcome sign of peace that Mr. George Orwell is able to publish his "fairy story" *Animal Farm*, a satire upon the totalitarian state and one state in particular' and Kingsley Martin, in *New Statesman and Nation* (1945) sees it as a 'gibe at the failings of the U.S.S.R.' and 'a bolt against Stalin'. Cyril Connolly, in *Horizon* (1945) reviews it as a 'devastating attack on Stalin and his 'betrayal' of the Russian revolution, as seen by another revolutionary', but continues, 'If Stalin and his regime were not loved as well as feared the Animal Farm which comprises the greatest land-mass of the world would not have united to roll back the most efficient invading army which the world has ever known.' He has obviously missed Orwell's real purpose. Rosenfeld, in *Nation*

(1946) views the allegorical aspect of the work as 'an exercise in identification' and refers to *Animal Farm* as 'a brief barnyard history of the Russian Revolution' but finds it disappointing in this respect; '*Animal Farm* should have been written years ago; coming as it does, in the wake of the event, it can only be called a backward work.' One of the best analyses of the fable as an allegory can be found in Jeffrey Meyers' excellent book *A Reader's Guide to George Orwell*, 'The political allegory of *Animal Farm*, whether specific or general, detailed or allusive, is pervasive, thorough and accurate, and the brilliance of the book becomes much clearer when the satiric allegory is compared to the political actuality. Critics who write, "it makes a delightful children's story" and who emphasize that "the gaiety in his nature had completely taken charge" are dimly unaware of the allegory's sophisticated art.' Meyers sums up *Animal Farm* in this way, 'Though subtle and compressed Animal Farm shares the serious theme of Nostromo: that once in power, the revolutionary becomes as tyrannical as his oppressor.'

Meyers sees the dark side of *Animal Farm*, viewing it as a vehicle for presenting a point of view and he sees this as having been successfully achieved – Rosenfeld sees it as unsuccessful and has to ask, 'What is the point of *Animal Farm*? Is it that the pigs, with the most piggish pig supreme, will always disinherit the sheep and the horses? If so, why bother with a debunking fable?' If it had been written before the event there would have been, he says, 'some value in the method'. Northrop Frye in *Canadian Forum* (1946) reviews the book as 'very well-written' and says that some of it 'is perhaps really great satire' but finds it generally inadequate, 'A really searching satire on Russian Communism . . .would be more deeply concerned with the underlying reasons for its transformation from a proletarian dictatorship into a kind of parody of the Catholic Church. Mr. Orwell does not bother with motivation: he makes his Napoleon inscrutably ambitious, and lets it go at that, and as far as he is concerned some old reactionary bromide like "you can't change human nature" is as good a moral as any other for his fable.' In *The Contemporary English Novel*, Frederick Karl considers that *Animal Farm* fails in its purpose 'by virtue of its predictability' – a point of view that is at odds with the concept of a fable as an inevitable movement towards a predetermined conclusion.

A reader has to make up his own mind how to interpret *Animal Farm* but a look at different interpretations will help to clarify and bring together formative impressions. An appreciation of the many different interpretations of the fable underlines the complexity and subtlety of so seemingly simple a work. It must be remembered, of course, that as the primary purpose of *Animal Farm* is political, the political persuasion of the reader, or his understanding of the events satirised in the fable, will influence to some extent the interpretation and appreciation of the satire.

REVISION QUESTIONS

The sections entitled Themes and Issues and Critical Appraisals should provide the student with many thinking points. The most important areas for revision could be covered by trying to answer the following questions.

1. What lie or lies does Orwell want to expose in *Animal Farm* and how does he get himself a hearing?

2. Is *Animal Farm* a successful fusion of the political and the artistic?

3. Does *Animal Farm* present the point of view that 'power corrupts, absolute power corrupts absolutely'?

4. Does *Animal Farm* embody Orwell's ideal that prose should be a 'window pane'?

5. Does *Animal Farm* present a pessimistic view of human nature?

6. To what extent is *Animal Farm* a satirical allegory on Russian history from the October Revolution to the Teheran Conference? How successful is this?

7. Is *Animal Farm* the history of a revolution betrayed or the intemperate rage of a disillusioned idealist?

8. Is the conclusion of *Animal Farm* an inversion of the tale's logic or is it symbolic of the animals' realisation of what has happened?

9. Is the moral of the fable that you cannot change human nature so things will always go badly?

10. What hope for the future does *Animal Farm* present or is it entirely pessimistic?

11. How is the satire *Animal Farm* controlled by humour – is this necessary or does it simply add to its charm?

12. Does *Animal Farm* fit the definition of a fable?

13. Does *Animal Farm* adopt the satiric formula – the corruption of principle by expediency?

14. If the events it is criticising have already happened, what is the relevance of *Animal Farm* today?

15. Do you think *Animal Farm* awakens the reader to social and political injustice or do you think the issues it presents are obvious already?

16. Selection is essential when presenting a point of view. Discuss the point of view of *Animal Farm* and how it is presented.

17. Does *Animal Farm* present the reason why dictators rise to power or does it just present an example of this happening?

18. What understanding of revolutions does *Animal Farm* encourage?

19. Is *Animal Farm* suitable as a story for children or is the subtitle misleading?

FURTHER READING

Biographical
Stansky, P. and Abrahams, W., *The Unknown Orwell*.
Crick, B., *George Orwell* (London, 1982).
Peter Lewis, *George Orwell: The Road to 1984* (London, 1981).

Critical
Jeffrey Meyers (ed.), *George Orwell: The Critical Heritage* (London, 1975).
Jeffrey Meyers, *A Reader's Guide to George Orwell* (Thames & Hudson, London, 1975).
Sandison, A., *The Last Man in Europe* (London, 1974).
Raymond Williams (ed.), *George Orwell: Twentieth-Century Views* (Englewood Cliffs, New Jersey, 1974).
Thomas, E., *Orwell* (London, 1965).
Zwerdling, A., *Orwell and the Left* (New Haven & London, 1974).